F.A.M.I.L.Y. Autism Guide
Your Financial and Day-to-day Blueprint for Autism

By Greg Zibricky
CFP®, ChFC, CLU, CASL

Dr. C. Dawn Zibricky
EdD, RN, PEL-CSN

ISBN: 978-1-733-8164-0-3

Provider Group Wealth Advisors
www.providergroup.com

FOREWORD

When our son was diagnosed with autism at the age of two, we decided to empower ourselves with knowledge and determination in an effort to help Antonio become the best person he could be. We began a journey of therapies and interventions, with the ups and downs expected from new parents who were learning and making mistakes on the way.

At that time we met Greg and Dawn Zibricky, parents of another wonderful boy with autism. Walking ahead of us on the same journey, the Zibrickys became a great source of solidarity and friendship, sharing their experiences and providing our family with a path of legal and financial interventions that gave us great peace of mind.

Today, almost 18 years later, we are fortunate to see and enjoy the results of all the love and work invested. Now we know that our son is going to be fine, and that in addition to being independent, which is always a work in progress, he is secure and protected in a clear legal and financial footprint that will be there even when we will no longer be around. The Provider Group is the best advice we can give to any parent starting the difficult, but highly rewarding journey of parenting a kid with disabilities.

Dr. Jose Penaherrera and Dr. Diana Jaime

PREFACE

Do you have a son or daughter, a friends or relative who is autistic? Do you feel confused? Unqualified? Overwhelmed? Are you reacting crisis-to-crisis instead of navigating a roadmap to the future?

F.A.M.I.L.Y. will serve to get you on track as Greg and Dawn Zibricky share their real-life situation by providing a step-by-step process to help families living with autism as they strive to navigate the future. Based on their oldest son's diagnosis twenty-two years ago and the challenges that diagnosis brought to their family, the Zibrickys share personal and practical knowledge to outline the specific plan needed to suit your particular family situation. In addition, they outline their achievements, their mistakes and the extraordinary circumstances you will probably encounter along your journey.

This revised edition of **F.A.M.I.L.Y.** includes two perspectives, incorporating the thoughts and expertise of both Greg and Dawn as they embarked on one of the most difficult struggles of their young lives—raising a child with autism at a time when autism was still an "unknown." They share their reactions to the initial diagnosis of their three-year-old son and its accompanying challenges, their fears and how their determination to confront that diagnosis changed their lives.

No two situations are identical, but the Zibrickys have experienced many of the challenges you might encounter. This book is their desire to assist families living with autism fine tune an individualized roadmap for their child's future.

What can you expect from **F.A.M.I.L.Y.?** You can expect answers to questions like:

- How can I be sure my child will be cared for when I'm gone?
- Where will my child live, work, play and worship™?
- How do government benefits work and how are they maintained?
- How can we avoid being disqualified from Federal or state benefits?
- What is the best way to save money for the future?
- What is the local school system required to provide for my child?

- What can I do as a parent to assist in my child's social development?
- How can I work with educators to assure my child receives the best education?

While this book might not be as much fun as spending a day at a spa, it will help you relax while throwing in a little bit of fun nonetheless. Loving families always do.

After reading F.A.M.I.L.Y. be prepared to:

- **Be more confident;**
- **Save money and time;**
- **Face new surprises daily without panic;**
- **Learn that autism is a mystery, with many kinds of solutions;**
- **Get started . . . NOW!**

ACKNOWLEDGEMENTS

To my wife Dawn whose dedication to our children, the nursing profession and the autism community has always been resolute.

To our son Benjamin, whose maturity, kindness and compassion have been awe inspiring.

Thank you to the Zibricky, Goehl and Roskamp families.

We both have worked and networked with a vast number of dedicated, hardworking parents, advocates and professionals. We applaud all of you for your strength and direction.

Special thanks to Terrie Varnet and Gene Rudnik who graciously took time to provide their experience and expertise.

Genuine appreciation is extended to: Rachael Roache for her assistance and patience in the development of this book; Mike Frantz for his valuable input and creativity; Dave Duncan for providing feedback and support; Ken Hawke at Star Visions Photography; and to the legion of therapists, aides, tutors and interested parties who have made vital contributions to Aaron's progress.

When this edition took on a broader perspective, we needed a second set of eyes for editing, corrections and suggestions. A very special thank you to our editor, Tonie Harrington. She understands the writing process and the difficulties that arise when trying to complete a project. Tonie can be reached at tonie.writingresources@gmail.com.

And from Dad to Aaron, who has changed my viewpoint on what heroism really means, and has changed our family in so many different and positive ways.

INTRODUCTION

We are probably the only authors on the planet who hope that their book becomes obsolete and irrelevant—and that it happens soon.

Our vision is that extraordinary day when scientists and brilliant medical minds come together to understand autism so well as to negate the need for the chapters and tips that follow in this book. Hopefully our politicians, legislators, representatives and educators will hear our voices loudly and clearly, thereby no longer neglecting the autism community. That would mean that every family raising a child anywhere on the autism-spectrum would have access to excellent, comprehensive medical coverage. We recognize that the current economy and political priorities in the United States might delay the coming of that day, but we can always hope!

Why have we chosen to re-write this book? Because we know there is a genuine need for it. Our oldest son Aaron has autism. We began our journey 22 years ago with his diagnosis at the age of three, and detailed planning for Aaron's future began in earnest a few years later. Many changes have occurred since the book was first published, and we want to address some of those changes.

We also felt the importance of including in this revised edition our experiences in raising Aaron in an environment that was ill-suited for rearing a child with autism. There were many social issues to address including the stigma placed on the "disabled," ignorance on the part of professionals as to what autism was, and teaching Aaron, as well as his fellow-students, how to communicate and work with each other.

In this book, we address specific situations that families like ours face without making broad generalizations. Most published materials about planning for the future are dreadfully generic or incomprehensibly large. We believe that there is a need for someone to speak *to* the autism community *from* the autism community. That is how **F.A.M.I.L.Y.** first came into being and that is what this Revised Edition represents—learning from those who have been there, who have walked the distance in search of answers.

We want to make the concepts as coherent as possible, removing the jargon and buzzwords you will undoubtedly hear on your journey of raising a child with autism. Instead we want you to learn in an uncomplicated way how clear-cut many aspects of future planning for your family can be.

The first portion of this book addresses the practical issues that parents of children with autism MUST face: How do you prepare for your child's financial future, and how do you find the resources to help your family now? We'll provide a real set of examples with real timelines and real lessons learned by us as Aaron has grown from age 3 to age 18 at the time of the initial writing, and then from 18 to 25 in this revised edition

Most of the ideas and actions in this book are not optional—**they are essential** for our families. Our intention is that after reading this **you'll be enabled** to make knowledgeable decisions because you are better informed and more confident. Just like any guidebook, you will find information to benefit everyone, even the most active and educated parents. By sharing our journey, hopefully you will pick out a few of your own mile markers and make your own course adjustments while taking a few scenic routes along the way!

Writing this book required looking back into family photos, videos, journals and other documents from the past 22 years. We've enjoyed that process. When we see the photos of our younger selves, we like what we see—a young, hopeful family ready to take on whatever life had in store for us. We've both moved forward since then, facing many obstacles. Hair color, weight and attitudes may have changed, however one bit of knowledge pulls it all together. We are more mature and wiser parents today, and we believe that our life together working to meet the challenges of autism has made us credible advocates for other parents of children with autism.

- **Greg and Dawn Zibricky**

TABLE OF CONTENTS

THE BEGINNING:

F.A.M.I.L.Y. FINANCIAL BLUEPRINT

22 YEARS AGO
. . . a Dad's recollection.

Sitting in the doctor's office on a chilly December morning, my wife Dawn and I stared at each other silently as the psychologist said, "Your son will never be able to own property. He may never be able to live on his own or have a job. Just keep him in school for as long as you can. He'll need their help and I believe by law they have to provide it. And it's a good idea to contact the State's Social Services Department to investigate the waiting list for residential homes. My jaw dropped. Dawn's hand tightened around mine.

Dawn and I had been married eight years and our first son, three and a half year-old Aaron, was not meeting his developmental milestones. Our second child, Benjamin, was eight months old at the time. I had left a large financial institution earlier that year to become an independent financial advisor. I earned the Certified Financial Planner certification and felt the only way I could do my job well was to work only for my clients and not a big corporation. Many friends and family members thought the move was foolish. *Greg, what will you do for a pension and medical benefits? How will you be able to distinguish yourself without a big company behind you?* I was 33 years old, healthy and ambitious. What could possibly go wrong?

Dawn worked as an Associate Professor of Nursing at a local university. Her maternal instincts and nursing background somewhat prepared her for our new reality. She didn't need tests and psychologists to tell her what to do for our son. As we left the doctor's office, Dawn's plan was in effect before we even reached the elevator doors.

My wife is a beautiful, intelligent woman who would stop at nothing to make sure our children reached their full potential, whatever that would be. As a father and husband, my first thought was, *"How do I fix this? How do I make this go away?"* Not so simple. My career had been spent helping people with their money, providing solutions and assisting clients in meeting their goals. This, however, was an unknown, so I immediately started looking for information and help.

I had no idea what to expect.

I was a freshman on the first day of school and I had not signed up for this class.

CHAPTER 1

F is for FLEXIBILITY

FLEXIBILITY IS DEFINED AS:

Capable of being bent, usually without breaking; easily bent
Susceptible to modification or adaptation; adaptable
Willing or disposed to yield; pliable

Something tells me that if the person who penned this description at Webster's had a son or daughter with autism the above definition would be three times as long. From experience, the moment your child is diagnosed your brain becomes wired for new challenges. They're coming and you know it.

Autism is not a "flexible" disorder. As any parent, sibling, teacher, or caretaker of an individual within the autism spectrum can tell you, flexibility and spontaneity are not in the dictionary of autistic life. However, as Aaron's parents, "flexibility" took on a myriad of new meanings the writers at Webster couldn't begin to imagine.

First, I had to become **Flexible in my Personal Interactions**. I had to learn to become less cynical and much more direct with my language. Nuance was out the window. My aversion to strict scheduling was also under attack. In my group of friends I was always the most restless—the guy who always thought there was something going on somewhere else that was more interesting than wherever I was.

I had to learn from the perspectives of others.

I had to learn to listen (and trust) the opinions of teachers and therapists.

I will always see my child through a specific lens—the lens of a Father. I cannot look at him through the lens of a doctor, a teacher or a grandparent. But I can learn from their lenses, from their various perspectives, to be a better parent, a better person.

Naturally, everyone sees things differently. Living in a family with autism, **we parents must be able to blend and bend our thinking to take**

advantage of how others can help us, and our child's circumstances. I might be an expert at financial planning, but I am not an expert speech pathologist.

I understand my limitations and have accepted them. It is critical that all of us as parents do the same. Self-awareness is the first step towards other-awareness and without truly understanding our own limitations we'll never properly understand those of our child.

Another lesson learned is that **without personal flexibility we can never see our child for who they really are**—and we'd miss out on so much joy and fun! Society has a view. So what? Let Aaron be Aaron.

Let your child be your child. If we try to "fix" them we are the losers.

So what if he or she is hugging telephone poles? So what if your kid loves vacuum cleaners? Typically children with autism have obsessions. Author Robert Eliot got it right when he said that Rule #1 is, ***Don't sweat the small stuff.*** When all you take with you is your memory and your character, and all you can impart to others is the same, embracing the uniqueness of each child is a joy and a privilege. Autism doesn't change that one iota.

As a toddler, Aaron's infatuation was ceiling fans. They became his obsession. Once at a hardware store, Dawn and I made the mistake of trying to hurry him past a spinning display of about fifteen ceiling fans. He erupted into panicked sobs. As Dawn consoled him, I noticed the confused stares of the workers and the scowls from parents who didn't know that Aaron had autism. Flexibility was needed—and quickly!—for us both to get over people's opinions and not care about what strangers were thinking.

Some years later while driving Aaron to the babysitter—a familiar route for us—we reached a construction zone. Instead of going straight ahead as usual, we took a left. Aaron mumbled from his car seat. I couldn't understand what he was trying to say. Later that evening Aaron walked around the house repeating, *"wrong way."*

That was my first realization of his absolute need for structure and my introduction to *echolalia*, which is the automatic repetition of vocalizations often associated with autism. The word *echolalia* comes from the Greek "echo" meaning repeat, and "lalia" meaning babbling, meaningless talk. Both of these situations presented Dawn and I with challenges to learn to be less rigid and more in the moment. They forced us to become **Flexible in our Personal Interactions**. As a result, we developed the following:

Top Tips for Flexible Personal Thinking:

1. Explore the 'What ifs'
2. Accept that rules, laws and life change
3. Realize that even "experts" don't know everything.

Flexible personal interactions and these three tips were essential—really the bedrock—in creating our own **F.A.M.I.L.Y. Blueprint**. Hopefully they will become your foundation in developing your own distinct plan and course of action for the future, while extracting as much joy and happiness along the way as possible.

Next, we had to learn to be Flexible in our Financial Decision Making. We learned that Flexibility, as it applies to financial matters, is primarily a state of mind. The point is to free yourself from misconceptions and nudge your thought process into a more fluid state. We all tend to think of financial decision making as a rigid world with no room for error or adjustment. It is exactly the opposite. For example:

The top excuses for avoiding Financial and Estate Planning are:

- **I don't know about it. I don't even know what to call it.**
- **I don't want to mess it up.**
- **I don't have any time.**
- **I don't have the money to meet with someone.**
- **I don't want to think about it. It's morbid.**
- **I'm TIRED!**

An example of poor flexibility in financial decision-making occurred during one of the more forgettable professional meetings in my career as a financial planner. I was leading an extended-family discussion. Things were going quite well and it seemed that everyone was on the same page until the patriarch rose from his chair and demanded silence. He shouted, "Everyone is trying to kill me!" Then he pounded his fist on the table and stormed out of the office. Not the best way to begin a dialogue. Well then, **how do you start?**

My first suggestion is to research the following:

Sensory Integration Therapy
Auditory Integration Therapy
Relationship Development Intervention (RDI)

Every family will need different resources depending upon what they value and where they are in their lives.

What do you value? Financial security? Independent living? Faith?

Aaron valued football—high school football. My wife and I agreed that one result would be forthcoming—Aaron would get killed! He, however, didn't see it that way. The team needed him and he needed them. The reasons were not all that obvious at the time. We were his parents, concerned about his well-being, and acceptance by teammates and acknowledgement of being part of a team didn't occur to us. Aaron, in the meantime, survived and thrived.

Our goal as parents has always been to maximize Aaron's full potential, whatever that might be, and to make every effort to meet his goals and dreams.

Another good suggestion to start the process is by conducting a MAP. MAP is a tool developed by Marsha Forest and Jack Pearpoint who also co-authored the book "All My Life's a Circle." MAP stands for Making Action Plans. It is designed to help individuals and families figure out how to move into their future effectively and creatively. It's a brilliant exercise for any kid and any family, and an especially amazing tool for children with autism. This process takes on added significance when the primary participant lives with autism where life can feel intensely unpredictable. 'Mapping' allows them to move into a future effectively and creatively—to quite literally get them from one place to another.

Aaron has had three MAP sessions over the years. For one of those sessions we decided to hire a moderator and an illustrator to take the pressure off the principal participants by having qualified intermediaries working with us. My entire career is based on that philosophy and it worked particularly well in helping Aaron also.

It is interesting to look back and see how one of those sessions was shaped and its results. Aaron sent an invitation to family, friends, neighbors, therapists, school aides and our pastor. The response was robust. Our home temporarily became a retreat center designed for participation from those who saw Aaron through a different lens than Dawn and I. Our parental day-to-day issues took a backseat.

Eighteen people gathered in a dining room with one thing in common—they all knew my son Aaron. Collectively, this group of people came from Aaron's life journey and included family members, his friends, teachers, past and current therapists and the minister from our church.

At center-stage was Aaron, talking about his hopes and dreams as he walked his life journey. Folding into the discussion were a myriad of folks who in some way wanted to help Aaron meet his future goals. Life is complicated, especially for a 13-year-old whose journey is about to include entering high school.

If there is one thing that **I have learned from Aaron,** it is that **when life seems complicated, we instinctively have the need to make it more predictable.** People, especially with autism, typically have this intense need for predictability. Going to high school when you've never been there before is scary. So these people from Aaron's journey in life came together to make that transition easier. This collaboration with people who knew Aaron the best was our greatest resource.

A MAP takes advantage of the visual tendencies of most individuals along the autism-spectrum. A MAP varies just as much as the individual who creates it, but it typically features several key components:

- **Hopes and dreams**
- **Current feelings**
- **Nightmares and fears**
- **Gifts and strengths**
- **Successes and**
- **Positive and possible future plans.**

It's a valuable tool to enable both the family and child with autism to look to the future.

Does your child's school offer this service?
Are there any professionals for hire in your area?

If not, here are a few **tips to help you do this on your own:**

- **Visit www.inclusion.com**
- **Get the book "All my Life's a Circle" by Falvey, Forest, Pearpoint & Rosenberg**
- **Invite the appropriate number of attendees to your MAP session**
- **Ask a trusted family member to conduct the proceedings**
- **Have an artistic friend create the illustrations**
- **Make sure the group is comprised of people with whom your child is comfortable**
- **Provide relaxed surroundings**

Optimism and interaction set the tone for that day. Aaron appeared happy, relishing others talking about his advances.

A sample of the results:

Dreams (Mission Accomplished!)

- Have a core of friends—good friends
- Live in a rural town—a place where it is not too loud
- Go to college—maybe in Austin, Texas
- Drive a car and cool trucks
- Always be involved in a faith community. (Aaron feels like he doesn't have autism when he's at church)
- Help others with disabilities and raise awareness and understanding

Nightmare (Fail the Mission!)

- Dreams quashed due to a lack of understanding
- People don't see gifts and talents—looked on as weird
- No advocates—unable to advocate for himself
- The bar will be lowered and not raised—a limited future
- Bullied by kids

- School says, "you can't be in this class"—prevented from experiencing an inclusive high school experience

We discussed the best possible future scenarios, focusing on what could be done to put and keep Aaron in a position to succeed.

What are your child's dreams?

What can get in the way?

Several of the items discussed during the MAP seemed particularly important at the time. Some continue to be, but others have faded.

So, what has happened in the area of autism between Aaron's diagnosis and today? **In 1996, the prevalence of autism was reported at 1 per 10,000 children** (Autism Science Foundation, 2018). Today those figures have changed to 1 in 59 births in 2018 (Center for Disease Control).

We are witnessing a significant rise in the prevalence of autism. At the same time a crisis exists in funding for services. This crisis will most likely get much worse. The impending multitude of adults with autism will need assistance. We see this first hand as we deal with Aaron's transition into adulthood.

What else has happened since Aaron was diagnosed? A few other events:

9/11	Internet Bubble Burst	Madoff, AIG
U.S. Invades Iraq	Cubs win World Series	Twitter/You Tube
Tsunamis, Earthquakes	U.S. Exits Iraq	LinkedIn/Facebook
Bush, Obama, Trump	Wi-Fi, Blogging	Enron, Lehman Brothers
Afghanistan	Real Estate Bubble Burst	White Sox win World Series

Things change. They always do. So stay Flexible.

CHAPTER 2

A is for ACCESS

<u>**ACCESS IS DEFINED AS:**</u>

1. The ability, right, or permission to approach, enter, speak with or use; admittance
2. The state or quality of being approachable
3. A way or means of approach

In this context, **access means our ability as parents or guardians to approach and use private and government solutions that exist (e.g. health care, insurance, etc.) to help our children live more fruitful and successful lives.**

As part of our responsibility for the health and well-being of our children, **we must educate ourselves on what options are available in both private and public sectors and work diligently to gain access to those options.**

When it comes to U.S. government support, however, at the initial printing of this book we saw a bit of divisiveness in the country with not everyone on the same page regarding government's responsibilities (versus the private sector) in providing support. A blog example from that time follows:

Why should the taxpayers pay for your child's services? Thievery in the name of autism is no less offensive than thievery of anything else. If you want services for autism than [sic] start a foundation. Rely on voluntary charitable donations. But don't use the heavy hand of government to force others to pay for your needs. Freedom is not free.

The point? **Don't assume U.S. government benefits and services are a given**. U.S. laws can and do change and you have to be prepared for these changes in the future to best assist your child. Care enough to be prepared. Over the 22 years since Aaron was diagnosed, we have seen a myriad of changes and expect to see more.

Remember to **also look outside of the U.S.** It's a flat world out there in more ways than one. Take advantage of expertise wherever you can find it.

Today there are three distinct issues to look at, and keep your eye on, in the area of Access, specifically regarding health care in America:

1. **Health Insurance**
2. **The Patient Protection and Affordable Care Initiative–2014**
3. **Medicaid**

The total estimated cost of health care for a family of four in a preferred provider plan (PPO) was recently quoted at $28,166 per year. (Milliman Medical Index, May 23, 2018) That's a staggering amount. The American Medical Association reported competition disappearing within the health insurance industry. The President of the AMA stated:

> *The near total collapse of competitive and dynamic heath insurance markets has not helped patients. As demonstrated by proposed rate hikes in California and other states, health insurers have not shown greater efficiency and lower health care costs. Instead, patient premiums, deductibles and co-payments have soared without an increase in benefits in increasingly consolidated markets.*

Even if you currently have the most comprehensive insurance to cover your family, as we've said, take care to **BE PREPARED**. It may not last forever. Companies are constantly adjusting benefit packages and looking for ways to cut increasing costs. And the rash of disturbing headlines highlights the continued challenge of gaining and retaining access to valuable services for our children with autism. For example, headlines in 2011 included "Fraying lifeline for struggling families" (*Chicago Tribune*), "Health Benefits costs rise most in six years" (*Bloomberg*). "Parents told to leave disabled kids at homeless shelters" (*Yahoo News*), and many more.

For example, in Indiana some parents testified that employees at the Bureau of Developmental Disabilities Services told them to leave their severely disabled children at homeless shelters if they could not afford to care for them. The parents were feeling the sting of a series of budget cuts to the Family and Social Services Administration and had made appointments to speak with the Bureau of Developmental Disabilities Services when they had failed to receive scheduled Medicaid waivers that paid to support disabled young adults to live on their own.

This speaks to two serious issues: 1) public employees not being properly trained in how to communicate to parents of developmentally disabled children (although that comment seems 'beyond the pale' of training); and 2) access to programs, as well as the actual programs themselves, can be cut or overloaded, based on political expedience at any time.

Lessons learned? First, always seek access to more than one public employee and preferably to a supervisor if you don't get the answer you are expecting. Second, be prepared with Plans b, c, and d if you are relying on an existing program, law, or bureau for support, because this support can be withdrawn as political will waxes and wanes.

In the case in Indiana, a spokesperson for the Bureau claimed that people were not waiting for their waivers any longer than usual and that workers who recommended parents to leave their children would be disciplined. But, advocates countered the Bureau's claims stating that the waiting list for the waivers had ballooned up to 20,000, and that 2,000 slots had vanished. A woman whose 22-year-old son has autism, epilepsy and attention deficit hyperactivity disorder stated: *"We are people and they are people. They have lives that are worth something."*

The frustration she felt and that we feel when we lack access or when it becomes uncertain can be extreme. For example, an article titled "Defining Essential Care" in the *Wall Street Journal* spoke to what services, therapies and care were truly needed and about the lobbying efforts underway by insurers. It featured a 5-year-old boy with autism and pointed out that the care he currently receives may not be covered under the new law. Ironically, the article was surrounded by ads for a jet leasing company, expensive suits/watches/shoes and a Jaguar XJ.

Our country is in a protracted dialogue regarding the proper balance of **what are essential services versus optional services** for its citizens, **and which of these should be taxpayer funded versus privately financed.** Leasing jets and buying expensive suits, watches and Jaguars are private expenditures and the government has no role in subsidizing or mandating their purchase or non-purchase, or in providing them to everyone. However, when it comes to health care and essential services to keep our citizenry healthy, it is quite a different question—one that will take long after this publication to be resolved.

Our recommendation is to be aware. Take care to be prepared. **Learn** what the accessibility is to options for your individual family circumstances. **Study** the issues to understand how you might be impacted if things were to change tomorrow. At no other time has self-awareness and "dirty-fingernail" research been more valuable to securing your child's future.

For example, the Department of Health and Human Services reported that more than 2.5 million adults younger than 26 were able to remain on their parents' health insurance plans because of a provision in new healthcare laws. The Affordable Health Care Act also ends the practice of denying young children insurance because of pre-existing conditions. By the time today's 19-year-olds reach 26 those rules will have been enacted for adults as well, according to Ron Pollack, the founding executive director of Families USA, a non-profit that works for health care reform for all Americans. See www.healthcare.gov for further details.

But this law could be repealed. Take care and be prepared. **Ask yourself these questions**. After age 26 comes and goes, or whenever my child falls off my medical plan,

- **Will s/he be able to get health insurance?**
- **Will s/he be able to afford coverage?**
- **Will s/he be able to manage it on their own?**

Regarding the changing landscape of health insurance, health care laws, Medicaid, and many other issues, most parents don't know where to turn. School systems and doctors' offices have been bombarded with questions that they are not prepared to or don't have the responsibility to answer.

The National Conference of State Legislatures, www.ncsl.org, breaks down the autism and insurance coverage laws state-by-state and provides additional resources.

Autism Votes, an Autism Speaks initiative, www.ausismspeaks.org, updates state and federal initiatives. Extremely proactive, its tagline is, ***"It's time for lawmakers to listen".***

If you happen to be dealing with an insurance company now and are having difficulties, then www.mhautism.org (Mental Health & Autism Insurance Project) is an excellent site to research. The Project founded in 2009 has as its mission "to assist families with children with autism spectrum disorders (and later other mental health conditions) to obtain medically necessary treatments through their health plans, so that they can ultimately reach their full potential."

As this revised 2019 edition goes to print, the current political landscape has vast potential implications on the future of health care, government benefits and the security of our children. The ACA, with its coverage of pre-existing conditions, is under enormous pressure. Supreme Court hearings are under way and local elections beckon. Deep division and uncertainty rule the day.

Our family goal early on was to make sure Aaron would be eligible for Supplemental Security Income (SSI) and Medicaid. It looked to be the best way for him to be assured of future health care assistance. Many professionals in our network shared this viewpoint.

For many of the families reading this, qualification to Medicaid will be essential. The following is from the Social Security website www.ssa.gov.

What is SSI?

"Supplemental Security Income (SSI) is a cash assistance program funded and administered by the Federal Government. The program is authorized by Title XVI (Supplemental Security Income for the Aged, Blind, and Disabled) of the Social Security Act. Beginning in January 1974, SSI replaced the Federal/State matching grant program of adult assistance to the aged, blind, and disabled. Under SSI, there is no minimum age limit for establishing eligibility based on blindness or disability.

Last Revised: Nov. 3, 2003"

Even though Social Security manages the program, SSI is not paid for by Social Security taxes. SSI is paid for by U.S. Treasury general funds, NOT the Social Security Trust funds. (Keep reading. I'll send hot tea and smelling salts.)

What do you need to specifically know about SSI for your child?

There are asset and income limits associated with the SSI program to which you must be KEENLY AWARE. Your young adult cannot have assets in their name greater than $2,000, nor make more than $1,010 per month. **If they exceed these amounts they WILL NOT BE ELIGIBLE for SSI because they will not be considered disabled.**

Make no mistake. If approved, **it is not just about receiving a supplemental check. It is about setting a precedent that will eventually get your child access into the Medicaid system IF he/she needs it.** This is an extremely important and essential point for you to understand:

YOU NEED TO CREATE A POVERTY MODEL AROUND YOUR CHILD.

For many families, unfortunately, this is not difficult. However, let's say that Aaron's Uncle Ned gives Aaron a check for $5,000. His chances of receiving assistance could now be destroyed, so loving attention from extended family members (even though reflected in gifts) can jeopardize your child's future. **It is essential that well-meaning family members understand that their intended kindness can actually be a detriment for your child obtaining the proper care and assistance s/he deserves.**

There are people not in our particular situation who ask: *"Well, isn't that 'gaming' the system?"* We respond that these are the rules and guidelines to work within, and ignorance of those guidelines should never be the reason why your child is denied critical services to which s/he has a right.

Another scenario. What if kindly old Uncle Ned just refuses to listen to you? The following sample letter can be used with Uncle Ned, family members or other interested parties who have made it known that they want to help, but simply aren't sure how to go about it.

SAMPLE LETTER TO WELL-MEANING RELATIVES AND FRIENDS:

Dawn and I are writing this letter to inform you of some very detailed planning that we have completed to protect Aaron's future. The work that we have done will protect Aaron's rights to qualify for public benefits to which he may be entitled, in the event that he is not able to be self-supporting in the workplace. Plans are not foolproof, and our plan is no exception. A well-meaning gesture could inadvertently disrupt our preparation and cause

Aaron to be ineligible for extremely important programs such as Medicaid and SSI. If your intention is to give anything of value to Aaron, we want you to know that:

- *Your intentions are welcomed and most appreciated; however,*
- *There is a very specific way to do it.*

The prerequisite is to be as specific as possible. Provide legal and tax counsel contact information when necessary. **Make doubly sure that all interested parties know that if they intend to give or leave anything to your child that it SHOULD NOT GO TO THEM DIRECTLY.** We'll discuss setting up a Third Party Special Needs Trust and its tax identification number later in the book.

It's also important for you to visit www.medicaid.gov and research your specific state of residence. Get the basic knowledge of what is available in your state. Many families we have known and worked with have moved to different states to receive better services for their child with autism. It is worth researching programs available in various states, particularly since all state landscapes are changing.

If you live in New York City, Atlanta, L.A., etc., you will have a different experience tracking down autism specialists and professionals than someone residing in a lightly populated rural area. This doesn't mean living in a big city will solve all of your problems, but your access to professionals will undoubtedly differ and perhaps also your access to high quality care. Many who are eligible for assistance and/or benefits do not apply because they do not know they exist or do not think their child is eligible for them. Remember:

DON'T LET IGNORANCE KEEP YOUR CHILD AWAY FROM SERVICES THAT ARE AVAILABLE TO HIM OR HER OR TO WHICH THEY ARE ENTITLED.

And above all, don't let social stigma get in the way either. You must make sure to get benefits wherever and whenever you can. For example, in Illinois there is a PUNS list at www.dhs.state.il.us. PUNS stands for Prioritization of Urgency of Need for Services. Aaron was on this list for a number of years. The list is comprised of people in Illinois with developmental disabilities who need services. Some of the services might include In Home Support, respite care, job coaches and group homes. It is well worth researching this program.

Remember – FOCUS ON ACCESS – and keep pushing.

CHAPTER 3

M is for MONEY

MONEY IS DEFINED AS:

1. Any circulating medium of exchange, including coins, paper money, and demand deposits.
2. Gold, silver, or other metal in pieces of convenient form stamped by public authority and issued as a medium of exchange and measure of value.

Time is money, cake, legal tender, bread, currency, the love of which is the root of all evil, dough, scratch, etc. The largest barrier to a successful plan is often the ability to finance it. **Children cost money, but autism is expensive—very expensive. Medications, therapies, special diets, alternative practices, transportation, and conferences all can put a massive dent in your savings account, retirement fund, or paycheck.**

In the beginning, after Aaron's initial diagnosis, Dawn looked at any and all promising programs. Unfortunately, our excursion into the world of therapies was largely an unknown adventure at the time. We are now well aware of the following: Applied Behavior Analysis, Relationship Development Intervention, Tomatis Listening Therapy, and Sensory Integration, and you may be also. If you are not, please look them up. (see Glossary)We won't spend time here describing them but understanding these therapies before you begin will save you valuable time in evaluating the best practitioners and assessing their likely effectiveness with your child.

The other major differences for parents and their children on the spectrum from the time of Aaron's diagnosis is the proliferation of adaptive technologies. In addition, exciting new sites and services are emerging all over the country.

After numerous trials, we found that intensive listening therapy seemed to help Aaron make better eye contact and become more socially engaged. Early in the process at a family party when we were discussing what was taking place, a friend of mine asked, *"Where's the data?"* That question rallied my senses and made me appreciate my wife's efforts even more. It became the turning point in how I would approach new and cutting edge therapies. No more quarrelling about funding. Time, determination, hard work, and results made every penny spent worthwhile. It started me thinking harder about money overall, how to protect Aaron, and how best to take care of him.

This section is NOT about specific investments or taxes. **It is about how normal money flows in a normal family**. It also concerns beneficiary forms and how assets are titled. You may say, *"I want to treat all my children the same."* **You can certainly treat them the same, however** when it comes to funding trusts and keeping assets in or out of an individual's name **you must be careful and cautious.**

Life Insurance	Primary Beneficiary	Relation	Contingent Beneficiary	Relation
Insured:				
Company:	Name:		Name:	
Policy #:	Address:		Address:	
	Phone:		Phone:	
Insured:				
Company:	Name:		Name:	
Policy #:	Address:		Address:	
	Phone:		Phone:	
Insured:				
Company:	Name:		Name:	
Policy #:	Address:		Address:	
	Phone:		Phone:	
Insured:				
Company:	Name:		Name:	
Policy #:	Address:		Address:	
	Phone:		Phone:	

Retirement Plans	Primary Beneficiary	Relation	Contingent Beneficiary	Relation
401(k) Plan:				
Company:	Name:		Name:	
Account:	Address:		Address:	
	Phone:		Phone:	
403(b) Plan:				
Company:	Name:		Name:	
Account:	Address:		Address:	
	Phone:		Phone:	
457 Plan:				
Company:	Name:		Name:	
Account:	Address:		Address:	
	Phone:		Phone:	
Keoghs:				
Company:	Name:		Name:	
Account:	Address:		Address:	
	Phone:		Phone:	
SEP:				
Company:	Name:		Name:	
Account:	Address:		Address:	
	Phone:		Phone:	
Defined Benefit/Pension Payments:				
Company:	Name:		Name:	
Account:	Address:		Address:	
	Phone:		Phone:	

Individual Retirement Account	Primary Beneficiary	Relation	Contingent Beneficiary	Relation
Owner:				
Company:	Name:		Name:	
Policy #:	Address:		Address:	
	Phone:		Phone:	
Owner:				
Company:	Name:		Name:	
Policy #:	Address:		Address:	
	Phone:		Phone:	
Owner:				
Company:	Name:		Name:	
Policy #:	Address:		Address:	
	Phone:		Phone:	
Owner:				
Company:	Name:		Name:	
Policy #:	Address:		Address:	
	Phone:		Phone:	
Owner:				
Company:	Name:		Name:	
Policy #:	Address:		Address:	
	Phone:		Phone:	

Other Plans & Contracts	Primary Beneficiary	Relation	Contingent Beneficiary	Relation
Deferred Compensation Plan:				
Company:	Name:		Name:	
	Address:		Address:	
	Phone:		Phone:	
Annuity:				
Company:	Name:		Name:	
Contract #:	Address:		Address:	
	Phone:		Phone:	
Disability Policy:				
Company:	Name:		Name:	
Contract #:	Address:		Address:	
	Phone:		Phone:	
529 Plans				
Company:	Name:		Name:	
Account #:	Address:		Address:	
	Phone:		Phone:	
Coverdell Education Savings Account:				
Company:	Name:		Name:	
Account #:	Address:		Address:	
	Phone:		Phone:	

- If Dawn is the primary beneficiary on my 401k, who should I name as contingent beneficiary?

This is where the "what if's" and questions come in.

- Don't I have to name all my children?
- Should I direct all the money to Aaron because he has a developmental disability?
- What about Benjamin?

Beneficiary forms will prevail. Don't be afraid of changing your mind. Compartmentalize assets, adjust percentages, do what you feel is appropriate, just **DO NOT leave money directly to your child living with autism.** An appropriate alternative will be discussed later.

Financial issues can intimidate some people, and that anxiety largely stems from the unknown. **Most people do not have an extensive background in financial and estate planning, cannot tell the difference between a term life insurance policy and a Power of Attorney**, and usually don't care—and that's okay! But, **when it comes to how to best take care of your child with autism, you need to be careful and pay attention.**

Imagine you have an intensely wicked toothache. You go to your dentist to get it checked out. Your dentist tells you that two wisdom teeth need to be taken out and proceeds to take out a saw and offers to do the procedure right then and there. More than likely you never heard the offer because you would have run out of the office with that goofy blue bib swinging from your neck the minute the saw made its appearance.

If you really needed that procedure, a general practitioner would refer you to an oral surgeon who would have the proper tools and appropriate skills to handle the job. A dentist knows what he can and cannot do. If only financial services operated in that manner. Unfortunately, **most "experts" in the financial services industry will never tell you they cannot do a service or provide a product, even if they have little or no understanding of it.**

Point? Watch out for the big blob of financial salespeople (fresh faced, nice crisp shirt) selling products under the guise of having

experience with autism. Dawn and I have met plenty of that breed.

A quick question to set further context on this issue—is one million dollars a lot of money? To many people the answer is an overwhelming YES! But wealth is relative, sometimes the more you have the more you feel you need. And these days it must be acknowledged that many people become angry or cynical about finance and money in general. They should be. The lack of regulation in certain financial markets has led to profiting by betting against our own financial system and way of life, and has caused tremendous harm on Wall Street and Main Street.

The best people in the financial planning profession provide an independent, unbiased perspective and are heavily regulated and scrutinized. They help clients understand how to stay on track during difficult times.

Three key money recommendations are:

1. **Keep an eye on budgeting and keep increasing the amounts you save.**
2. **Don't ever stop saving because of circumstances you cannot control. You can control the level of monthly savings. You cannot control the price of gas.**
3. **Tailor expectations, sacrifice when possible and remain positive.**

I know many of you are looking at the tips and shaking your head. If only it were so easy. Well, I am going to go out on the limb and be the bad guy here. There is no easy way of saying this, but **if you don't have money you NEED TO GET IT.** Raise it, create it, find it, earn it, and do whatever you have to so its there when it's needed.

I can hear the blog backlash now. *You're killing me!* I'm living paycheck to paycheck as it is. OK, what is your cell phone bill? Cable? How much are you saving? **It's time to scrutinize every single item if you haven't already done so. And once you've done that, do it again.**

Another aspect of money management that can be particularly helpful for families with a child with autism is "gifting." Most people think of gifting as a rich man's exercise. But, what if your extended family bought a life insurance policy on you? A truly different approach that may well be a very supportive birthday or holiday gift, right? What if they assisted with educational costs and therapies not covered by insurance?

Have you considered charitable gifts to organizations that serve and support your child? The global financial crisis over the last several years has reminded us about the importance of cash flow. Charities have suffered and services have been cut dramatically

Then there's ABLE. In 2014 a measure was passed by Congress and signed into law that allows eligible individuals with disabilities and their families to establish a tax-exempt savings account for expenditures that fall under "qualified disability expenses." **The Achieving Better Life Experience Act (ABLE Act) allows for education, personal support services and aids for employment, among other expense criteria.** Over the past few years various state legislatures have authorized the creating of the ABLE account savings programs. Similar to a state's 529 college savings program, the ABLE accounts are overseen by a state's treasury office.

An ABLE account is something I consider a "living support" program put in place by a family to strengthen other assistance the individual receives. There are limits on how much an ABLE account can accumulate before it would impact a beneficiary's SSI cash benefit.

By recent count on the **Saving for College** website there are 36 states and the District of Columbia which offer an ABLE account. Some states only allow participation by a resident of the state, while other programs are open to all US residents. The programs vary as far as cost of maintaining an ABLE account and the features such as a Debit Card, so comparison shopping is advised. Another alternative is the Advisor-Directed ABLE America account offered by Virginia 529 and American Funds.

A valuable resource for information on ABLE accounts is the ABLE National Resource Center (ANRC) founded by the National Disability Institute. The ANRC provides information on ABLE accounts to many stakeholders, such as federal and state agencies, financial institutions and individuals in the disability community. Their website is www.ABLENRC.org.

It's not about how much money you have, but what that money produces on a consistent basis. If you don't have enough money to secure a possible long-term cash flow need (and most people don't), you'll want to create leverage.

CHAPTER 4

I is for INSURANCE

INSURANCE IS DEFINED AS:

The act, system or business of insuring property, life, one's person, etc., against loss or harm arising in specified contingencies, such as fire, accident, death, disablement, or the like, in consideration of a payment proportionate to the risk involved.

Parents of children with autism are generally so overwhelmed dealing with issues that fill their time every day of every week of every year, that their schedule rarely allows time to think about the future. **We owe it to ourselves and our children to be proactive in our thoughts and put aside time on a consistent basis.** Our kids have hopes and dreams. Proper preparation and appropriate funds will help in making those dreams come true.

In a 2010 *USA Today* article entitled "Millions of Families Missing Safety Net," it was reported that the number of U.S. families without life insurance is at an all-time high. Only 44% of households have an individual life insurance policy and a staggering 30% have no individual or employer-provided policy.

The article cites the economic downturn and procrastination as the top reasons for these massive oversights. Most families said they haven't purchased life insurance because they "have other financial priorities;" yet, families with children under 18 "would have immediate trouble paying expenses if their primary breadwinner died." Why do we insure our cars and homes appropriately but not ourselves?

As the *USA Today* article illustrates, people—especially young people—tend to opt towards the cheapest plan because their health is not an issue at the time that they are purchasing their policy. However, as they age or if they are confronted with an unexpected illness, they cannot afford to make a commitment to coverage. **Protect your spouse and your retirement. It's not an either/or proposition.**

One question that arises is how do we plan for such a potentially

long time frame? There is no reason most of our children with developmental disabilities will not live a full life. Years ago, Dawn and I looked at how much Aaron's actual expenses were and developed a financial needs analysis. The projected need at that time was to cover a minimum of $1,700.00 per month based on the actual costs at that time. What if it's 30 years? 40? 50? That's a lot of zeros! **IT IS NEVER ENOUGH. However, don't let that stop you. Make your decisions within your individual budget and do the best you can.**

Insurance comes into play in long-term planning for the well being of your child. **Life insurance is considered by many to be the only asset that can generate tax-free dollars exactly at the time most needed.** Not many other savings or investment vehicles can provide that type of utility. By providing for the funding of a trust with life insurance, other assets can be allocated for your retirement income. Creating additional income sources will provide flexibility to assist other family members or charitable organizations.

Perhaps the most useful form of life insurance in terms of leverage and trust efficacy is survivorship universal life, also called "last-to-die" life insurance. Survivorship life insurance is purchased on two people, typically a married couple, and the death benefit is paid on the last of the couple to pass away. Insuring two lives with only one death benefit is less expensive, sometimes as much as 20% to 30% lower than covering a single life.

When recommending a survivorship universal life policy, the expectation is that children with special needs will outlive their parents. This method of funding a special needs trust (SNT) happens when both parents have passed away. Special needs trusts are highly effective with good leverage and protection of benefits for the named child.

When it comes to marketing, don't be confused by names of life insurance policies. There are only three chassis—three different ways you can construct a contract. They are **Term**, **Universal Life** and **Whole Life**.

Ignore all the other terms like single premium, equity linked, blended, dividend paying, and on and on. All you need to know are those three types of contracts.

TERM

Term provides the largest death benefits with the least amount of cost. The following charts show sample premiums by gender, age, approval rating and time frame.

Term Life Rates

Annual Premiums for $1,000,000 of **10 Year** Level Term Coverage

	Male			**Female**		
Age	Preferred Nonsmoker	Standard Nonsmoker	Standard Smoker	Preferred Nonsmoker	Standard Nonsmoker	Standard Smoker
25	$312	$529	$1,050	$239	$427	$600
30	$312	$529	$1,060	$239	$436	$770
35	$329	$533	$1,490	$277	$437	$1,190
40	$440	$734	$2,100	$379	$639	$1,750
45	$714	$1,170	$3,400	$610	$939	$2,720
50	$1,103	$1,867	$5,611	$913	$1,395	$3,145
55	$169	$2,887	$8,345	$1,350	$2,006	$5,178
60	$2,834	$4,452	$12,720	$2,024	$2,981	$8,355
65	$5,328	$7,911	$20,385	$3,245	$4,606	$12,425

That pricing gets locked in for the duration of the contract. No cash value. No death benefit if you live too long. This approach works particularly well for families on a budget, whether there are disabilities or not. It is the preferred way to have each spouse protect each other during the time the mortgage is large and the kids are small.

When it comes to funding a trust, the ONLY acceptable result we are looking for is that the insurance is in force when you die.

UNIVERSAL LIFE

With Secondary Guarantees/Lifetime no-lapse rider

WHOLE LIFE

Both Universal Life and Whole Life can be structured to cover an individual or a couple (survivorship). Age, health and hobbies will alter the rates, and family circumstances will affect the decision-making process.

The main point to remember is that the decisions made MUST BE

SUSTAINABLE. Overzealous salespeople and emotional purchases must be avoided. Think about year eight or year 28 of the policy, not the signatures or the first payment. The level of savings to be used and the future budgeting for permanent policies should emanate from an unadventurous mindset. It is important that you build on the planning and not overcommit.

What if the uncertainty over costs and timing is overwhelming? Buy term insurance with convertibility options. That allows you to lock in your health status and switch to a permanent policy later.

PROVIDE CARE FOR LIFE™

Acquiring insurance coverage makes a lot of people uneasy. Whether it's talking with agents, not being comfortable with the subject, or not having the time, it is not their strong suit.

Today the life insurance marketplace is ultra competitive. This provides access to hundreds of companies and more flexibility in tailoring an appropriate portfolio of benefits. Calculating needs, shopping and applying for coverage is easier now than ever before.

There is one more extremely important tip regarding life insurance that needs mentioning at this time.

If you have an existing cash value contract(s) you have got to get an In-force Illustration. This will show you what is happening today moving forward, and not what you think you bought or what the original illustration says.

Older Universal Life policies from long ago did NOT have secondary guarantees and lifetime no-lapse riders. It is critical that these contracts are reviewed. Interest rates have had a steady decline for many years. Do yourself a favor and learn what you REALLY own so there are no surprises.

Here are a couple of life insurance organizations that have calculators and/or evaluation services:

Consumer Federation of America: www.consumerfed.org
Life Happens: www.lifehappens.org

CHAPTER 5

L is for LEGAL

LEGAL IS DEFINED AS:
Appointed, established or authorized by law; deriving authority from law

This section contains responses from professionals in the legal field with terrific legal minds to questions raised by the author for this book. It's a Q & A of sorts with experts in the legal field—attorneys who are far more apt to recommend someone to do a task that is not their specialty than other professionals might be. They'll tell you it's not their forte and happily give you the name of a colleague who can help you.

In 2003 Dawn and I decided to amend our existing Wills and create a Third Party Special Needs Trust on Aaron's behalf. Properly drafted, this document would protect Aaron and provide us with peace of mind upon leaving the planet. At that time we were introduced to Eugene Rudnik, who had been a licensed attorney in Illinois since 1974. His practice included banking and general corporate law, estate planning and probate, which included planning for families with a disabled family member. Gene drafted his first special needs trust in 1993 and has worked in that area continually since then.

Q1: Gene, what usually stops parents from doing what they need to do?
A1: It's a reluctance to prepare for their inevitable deaths. With respect to their disabled child, parents typically either do not have sufficient information or don't know where to turn for sound advice. As a result, they feel helpless so they do nothing."

Q2: Once my son's Special Needs trust is completed, can I change it?
A2: The Special Needs Trust is typically irrevocable, which means that it cannot be changed or modified once it is completed. That does not mean that you and Dawn cannot change the successor trustees. In fact, you already have. Originally upon death or disability your brother and an

independent trust company were named. The trust company was bought out and your brother now has his own children so we amended the trust. The authority to amend the Special Needs Trust is, however, limited.

Q3: Why do I need a special needs trust?
A3: When a Special Needs Trust is properly drafted, any assets in the trust will not cause a problem with government benefits (SSI, Medicaid). For example, normal assets in Aaron's name in excess of $2,000 will result in the termination or reduction of SSI and Medicaid benefits. In addition, Medicaid may reclaim from his assets reimbursement for medical care provided. The Special Needs Trust, when properly drafted, avoids this situation. If the Special Needs Trust exists it can be funded and used now. Anyone, except the person with a disability, can make deposits into the Trust. This is a much better option than writing a testamentary trust inside a will. The Trust needs to state that it is not intended to replace government benefits. If there is any question as to the use of the funds in the Trust, check with Social Security and Medicaid.

The trust we created is titled:

Gregory and C. Dawn Zibricky, Trustees

Aaron Paul Zibricky Supplemental Needs Trust, Dated 2/27/2003

- How will the trust for your child's benefit be titled?
- Who will act as trustee when you are no longer able?
- How do you select trustees?

The visual that may come to mind when hearing the words "trust department" or "trustee" probably consists of huge chandeliers, marble floors and imposing secretaries. The good news is that the trust "business" is more accessible than ever before. We decided upon having co-trustees. The current plan includes a responsible family member who knows Aaron very well and a professional trustee to handle accounting and appropriate distributions.

Remember Flexibility? This decision is not carved in stone.

What if you have . . .

- Limited resources?
- Emergency circumstances?
- A lack of family choices for trustee or co-trustee?

Another alternative is a special planning technique called a pooled trust. These trusts pool resources of many beneficiaries and are managed by a non-profit association. Directories of pooled trusts are available through The Academy of Special Needs Planners, The Special Needs Trust Administration, and The National PLAN Alliance.

Remember the beneficiary discussion? Many families consider the job done once the trust is drawn up. WRONG! Once the trust is established, assets must be properly titled and beneficiary designations updated.

Guardianship

In many years of working with families affected by autism the most emotional issue parents dwell upon is whether or not to seek guardianship. Parents of young children contemplate what will happen when their child turns 18 and they are no longer the legal guardians. As children reach their teenage years, the issue becomes even more daunting.

Guardianship is a legal means of protecting children and incompetent adults who cannot take care of themselves, make decisions that are in their own best interest, or handle their assets due to a physical or mental disability. When the court determines that a person is incapable of handling either their personal and/or financial affairs it appoints a guardian. In Illinois and several other states, the person who is disabled is referred to as the "guardian's ward." Other terms to reference the person adjudicated as incompetent are used in different states. For example, Massachusetts refers to a "protected person" rather than a ward.

It became obvious as Aaron neared high school that he would be able to advocate on his own behalf in various instances of decision-making. We knew he would stay in the school system beyond high school, potentially until age 22. Aaron wanted us to continue helping with school matters,

I.E.P's and advocacy. Dawn and I were also concerned about Aaron's aversion to medical procedures, especially needles. We turned to a long-time trusted advisor, attorney Theresa Varnet, for answers. Her law firm—Spain, Spain and Varnet, P.C.—is well known and provides services in Illinois and Massachusetts. Terrie has been a tireless advocate for persons with disabilities for more than 40 years.

Our family discussions and Terrie's consult led to the creation of three distinct documents:

- **Durable Power of Attorney for Health Care**
- **Durable Power of Attorney for Property and,**
- **Durable Power of Attorney for Advocacy**

Q) Terrie, would you please tell us more about these less intrusive alternatives to Guardianship?

A) The upside to these alternatives is that no rights are taken away from your child. The downside is that no rights are taken away! The only "power" one has with a Durable Power of Attorney is removing the barrier of confidentiality. With the POA, you can attend meetings, as well as review and release records. However, when it comes to Aaron, the only power you have 'over' him is the power of persuasion. He retains all rights and powers and can withdraw the POA at any time or refuse to follow your advice. While no one option is perfect, the POA is a less expensive and less intrusive alternative to guardianship.

Q) Terrie, we have already used the advocacy power in recent sessions with the Department of Human Services and in Aaron's last I.E.P. What other alternatives to Guardianship do you see used by families touched by autism?

A) Trusts may be an appropriate alternative to appointment of a Guardian in some circumstances. A joint bank account that requires two signatures on any check can be created to prevent rash disbursements.

Q) What about finding appropriate counsel in rural or less populated areas of the country?

A) The Academy for Special Needs Planners, www.specialneedsanswers.com and The Special Needs Alliance, www.specialneedsalliance.org provide lists of Special Needs Planning Attorneys throughout the United States.

I cannot stress enough the importance of appropriate legal and estate planning. Throughout my 33-year career I have seen, too many times, the failure to protect a disabled individual, and have seen the tragedy and unexpected consequences of reactive situations.

They haunt me.

CHAPTER 6

Y is for YELL, YAK, YAP

YAP IS DEFINED AS:
To talk, especially uninterruptedly and idly; gab; chatter

YAK IS DEFINED AS:
Trivial or unduly persistent conversation

One area that Dawn and I have always been passionate about is recording information. Who else would have a clue about what we were doing for and with Aaron if tragedy struck? It can be valuable to put any desired future care instructions in writing, or on video.

The Live, Work, Play, Worship™ section in the back section of this book is extremely easy to fill out and will help provide guidance to those who fill your shoes if unfortunate and unforeseen events unfold. Though it will not take the place of legal documents, it can help fill in the gaps between those papers and more abstract concepts, like how and where you would prefer to have your child raised. It has spaces for the names of your child's therapists, information on their favorite activities, religious preferences and more. It is a simple tool to help you see the broader picture and further ensure that your child will be raised the way you want in the event you pass away or become disabled yourself. It also works as a living document.

We have always been EXTREMELY PROACTIVE in helping Aaron create friendships and community contacts. It was important for us to know the extended families of his acquaintances and maintain contact on a consistent basis. Write it down. Expand upon this at your discretion. Ample space to develop your own Journal is provided but don't stop there! Keep writing. Keep thinking. Keep updating. Get the i-Pad or video camera out. Have fun.

Remember—the more information you have for yourself, potentially the more you can leave for future guardians, caretakers and trustees.

I expect your first question is, "Where do I start?" Remember the MAP? You can use your most recent version as a guide for what works and what doesn't.

A big part of our family's communication was to do presentations. Dawn and I have spoken, together and separately, at many dozens of events. Our public outreach achieved a high point when Aaron, Dawn and I spoke at the National Conference of The Autism Society of America in Scottsdale, Arizona.

Our son Benjamin came with us. Our niece Jami came with us. Associates and friends joined us in the desert. We had a posse. Temple Grandin walked by. We were going to change how families like ours would see the future. The title was "Look out Future, Here I Come!—Understanding Person-Centered Planning, Financial Planning and Documentation."

I love the desert, even the hot blow dryer that is July in Arizona. At dinner one evening I recall being surrounded by our very supportive group. It should have been a celebrated moment. My perception was that I hadn't done anything yet. Up until that point in time that's how it had always felt to me. *Ask questions Greg. Ask more questions Greg.* What was the point of this exercise? Was it really going to help Aaron? Would this process help me to help him? I didn't have an answer.

It was autism 24/7. It wasn't healthy and the toll was mounting. I had not realized the pressure that was building. As Aaron readied for high school it became obvious that we had to back away from what we were doing. Dawn would go back to teaching and concentrate on finishing her doctorate. I would focus on my wealth advisory business.

Flash! Four years later. High School and I.E.P's and Graduation!

An area of autism that is only just starting to be explored is preparing yourself and your child for their transition into adulthood. If your child is approaching high school age, you will start to hear parents complain about the new, unexpected challenges they have to face. Without a support system, this period in life can be extremely stressful for parents as they are faced with new challenges such as employment, transportation, housing and more. A great site to visit and network is www.autismafter16.com. You can read articles written by adults with autism, professionals in the adult services and watch videos to help teach your young adult new skills for their new life. The site stresses the importance of thinking forward and being proactive.

Many young adults are creating self-advocacy websites and blogs. They are creating businesses. It is easier today than ever before to find intriguing and inspirational success stories. So much has changed since I started working with our population. Without social media I would not have found out about Jasper Steed, Paul Isaacs, Thokil Sonne or the Autistic Self Advocacy Network.

Another area of great importance for Dawn and I was the employment opportunities we desired for Aaron after college. We worked with Aaron on many areas (education, transitioning, interviewing) to help him prepare for stepping out on his own. We are very pleased with how he was able to move from college into a position that matches his college studies and interest. With this job come the benefits and satisfaction from being part of a work team supporting his community where he grew up.

Many individuals in the autism community are recognized for their unique capabilities in the workplace. It sometimes takes a bit (or a lot) of extra effort for business leaders and employers to make access a reality. The goal of many advocates is to spread the word about our kids, telling everyone what they are capable of.

One of these organizations is Autonomy Works (www.Autonomy.Works). Their goal is to shake open access to opportunities for individuals with disabilities. Autonomy Works provides its clients with marketing operations support employing staff members who are on the autism spectrum. Clientele are located throughout the U.S. and abroad. Autonomy Works stresses how several other similar organizations provide a wide-range of business services with the assistance of employees who have intellectual or physical disabilities. The need is certainly there.

Another leader in the field of disability inclusion is **ADVICE** (www.Autism-Advice.org). **ADVICE** is a partnership between NEXT for AUTISM, Autism Speaks, key businesses and community organizations, and a team of National Business/Disability Consultants. The team at **ADVICE** includes Meg O'Connell and James Emmett, both well-known leaders in disability inclusion. They will assist companies with autism hiring initiatives that will build a diverse labor and customer pool of dedicated employees.

There's an app for that!

Where?

Autism Speaks Financial Planner is a brand-new app that was released as this original guide was being completed. It was created to help you find information on financial resources and provides tools that can help pave a secure future for your child. I can't wait to dig in!

As parents, Dawn and I have been incredibly fortunate to have our particular skill sets. And as hard as this jaunt has sometimes been, we realize it could have been much more difficult. When the first edition of **F.A.M.I.L.Y.** was written, Aaron and I sat to discuss the book project. Aaron's responses from that discussion are as important today for parents of children with autism, as they were then for Dawn and myself. Ironically that same day the *New York Times* ran an article by Benedict Carey entitled "New Definition of Autism Will Exclude Many, Study Suggests."

Aaron! You are cured! We laughed.

Here is our conversation.
Q1: What are the biggest differences between being a kid and being 18?
A1: "Becoming an adult and I want to go to college and find a job."

Q2: What is something common that people don't understand about autism?
A2: "My thoughts are mine. I'm not stupid."

Q3: What challenges have you had to face?
A3: (High School to College) "Going through a lot of changes. I don't want to be left behind."

Q4: What do you see yourself doing 10 years from now?
A4: "Hopefully things will run smooth and I can find a business job. I want to help people."

Q5: Where do you think you'll live later in your life? You used to think it would be a rural area. Quiet.
A5: "I'm losing touch with the country. People tell me I'm a human GPS! I like to go everywhere. I'd probably like to live in the suburbs like we do now. I can visit the city or the country."

Q6: Because Mom (Dawn) grew up in a farming community you were exposed to organizations like 4-H and the Future Farmers of America. That seemed to be very helpful in creating a solid work ethic. How do you like your part-time job?
A6: "I like my job at the grocery store. I work hard, I don't stand around and I keep moving. I don't know what field I want to get into. I could help people with their money like you!"

Q7: There is an excellent guidebook called "Making Self Employment Work for People with Disabilities" by Cary Griffin and David Hammis. Do you have any thoughts or ideas about starting your own business?
A7: "I like food! I don't know."

Q8: You've always wanted to help other kids like yourself. Do you believe your desire to have these discussions and put yourself "out there" will help a lot of people?
A8: I hope so.

ONWARD

IN CLOSING

The following letter from me to Aaron was part of the first edition of this guide, and I want to include it again here.

Dear Aaron,

I am very proud of you. Thank you so much for making this journey of ours so gratifying. You have become a fine young man—a young man who has endured much. The future will be challenging as well, but you have raised the bar at every turn and I believe you will continue do so.

I'm glad I signed up,
Love,
Dad

P.S.: Now turn off the video game and get some sleep!

F.A.M.I.L.Y.

Day-to-day Blueprint

22 Years Ago
. . . A Mom's recollection

The Day of Never

"Mr. and Mrs. Zibricky, your son has severe autistic tendencies. As you know, he has very little language, odd behaviors and does not give much eye contact."

On a dark blue carpeted floor of a psychologist's office in Chicago, Illinois, my son Aaron stares at the toys placed in front of him. Seated parallel and above Aaron in a padded brown leather office chair, a near 60-year-old bearded male psychologist sat with the latest version of the *Diagnostic and Statistical Manual for Mental Disorders IV* opened up on his lap.

"Children with autism usually see you as nothing more than an object. He may never come to know you as his mother." The psychologist stopped and looked at me for some kind of response.

I was quiet and did not respond.

In a slow but steady voice he continued, "Autism makes it difficult for a mother to bond with her child." He paused again. "I know you will want to give him all the help he needs but he may resist you; this is because oftentimes children with autism are 'off in their own little worlds.'" The psychologist continued, "He will probably never be able to work or own property. So, it will be a good idea to contact the state's social services department to begin to investigate the waiting list for residential living. Chances are he will never be able to live on his own."

I tried to listen. My conscious mind was working hard to purposefully pay attention to what the psychologist was saying. However, the words "he will never" kept intruding upon my thoughts. My throat began to tighten and my chest started to hurt. I felt like I couldn't breathe as if I were drowning. My body was still, but my mind was racing with the words over and over "he may never know you as his mother."

There was silence in the room once the psychologist stopped talking. I found myself staring at him as he looked at me for some kind of a response. After a few silent moments, I slowly got up from my chair and headed toward Aaron sitting at the psychologist's feet. I gently picked him up and caressed him to my chest. His legs involuntarily wrapped around my waist. I held his body close to mine with one arm around his hips and my other hand cupping the back of his head. I gently kissed him on the cheek as a warm steady flow of tears streamed down my face.

> My husband Greg gathered up our belongings and without saying a word, we left.
> It was a quiet walk down the hall.

As we entered the elevator, I handed Aaron over to Greg. I was shaking. With my face in my hands, I collapsed down upon my knees and began to sob. "No way." I mumbled. "No way." I looked up at Greg and I could see Aaron looking down and reaching toward me. I took Aaron back and sat down on the elevator floor holding him. "He *will* know that I am his mother," I cried. "He already does!"

Greg sat down beside us. He held Aaron and me in his arms. "Yes," he whispered gently. "He does know you . . . and I suspect someday he will own his very own condo."

CHAPTER 7

F is for FACTS

I want to stress the importance of statistics in 1996, when Aaron was diagnosed with autism, that showed the prevalence of autism at **1 per 10,000 children** (Autism Science Foundation, 2018). As we now know, that figure **has risen to 1 in every 59 births** in the United States (Center for Disease Control [CDC]).

The first edition of this book focused on financial planning for children with autism, as does the first half of this revised edition. However, my focus addresses how we worked toward enabling Aaron to meet his future goals on a day-to-day basis. Our emphasis as parents, family, friends and professionals has always been to recognize Aaron's dreams and goals for the future. To achieve that, we had to recognize the challenges he would face personally and socially.

I'm writing first about the facts because **I believe all parents, professionals and family members must pursue accurate and current information.** Planning for the future of a person with autism **requires knowing the best approaches** available to assure that successful and meaningful future.

I am a nurse and mother. Reading and researching numerous articles has taught me to find the most reliable information based on evidence. To a parent new to the diagnosis of autism for their child, the world seems to spin out of control. *Why did this happen? What did I do? What can I do now? Where do I go?*

As a start, you can turn to reputable sources such as the Center for Disease Control (CDC), the Autism Society of America (2016), Autism Speaks (2018) and the Interagency Autism Coordinating Committee (IACC) from the U.S. Health and Human Services Department (2018). (Further contact information is located in Resources at the back of this book).

The IACC authorized by the Autism CARES Act passed in 2014 convened to begin a strategic plan that would continue investigating the science behind autism (quantitative research), and the actual lived experiences of individuals within the autism spectrum (qualitative inquiry). The findings and outcomes from the Autism CARES Act are now being published, and that's an exciting breakthrough for those of us who are part of the autism community.

As a parent, I am truly moved by the years of dedication given by professionals working on the IACC to learn more about autism, including investigating hereditary genes, genomics (the inter-relationship of genes and their influence on growth and development), brain imaging, and brain chemistry. More impressive **is that research and inquiry is now investigating ways to promote assistance for activities of daily living—the social aspects of life including supporting higher education, employment, dating, sex, getting married, and living the life that individuals with autism wish for themselves.**

Over the course of the last twenty years, attitudes related to how we speak about persons with disabilities have changed, depending upon the audience. The most common language to use today is **"People-First Language"** (The Arc, 2018). For example, instead of saying "a Down Syndrome student," we would say "a student with Down Syndrome" because that **minimizes the labeling**. My son Aaron prefers to drop labels altogether. He is a student. In his mind, autism is simply a part of his health and social history needed for documentation in the medical and educational arenas. In my professional capacity as a public speaker covering various disabilities, I go to great lengths to find out prior to a speaking engagement or written article what language is preferred and how to best meet and respect the preferences of the audience.

For clarification in this book, I will use the current language of Autism Spectrum Disorder (ASD) to explain the changes taking place in society. The word "autism" will be used when reflecting on older stories, since it was commonly used in an older historical timeframe. It is important to clarify the terminology surrounding the use of autism labels. For years many terms encompassed the description of autism, depending on the medical literature or the organizations talking about autism. The most commonly used terms of the past included: Autism; Pervasive Developmental Disorder (PDD); Pervasive Developmental Disorder—Not Otherwise Specified (PDD-NOS); Autism Spectrum Disorder (ASD); and, Asperger Syndrome. That's a lot of terms to describe the symptoms of one disability.

Recently, the Diagnostic and Statistical Manual of Mental Disorders put out its 5th edition (DSM-5) and made a major change by dropping the diagnosis of Asperger Syndrome and changing the psychological term to Autism Spectrum Disorder. The intent was to send the message that there is a range of abilities. Not everyone agreed with this change, and it proved to be confusing for some individuals who prefer the term Asperger's. As a result, several support groups and a worldwide network of individuals who call themselves "Aspies" came into being. Like other movements in society, Aspies are proud of who they are. They connect socially on-line and have developed several systems of support (The Asperger/Autism Network, 2018).

I am excited for children with autism and their families as they will be the beneficiaries of new technologies on brain imaging, better treatments, and exciting findings both in the field of genetics and genomics. Genetics (the study and function of genes) has been around for over a century, and Genomics looks at how complex biological systems such as the brain and many other systems function. The Human Genome Project (HGP) started in the 1990s as a collaborative effort between the National Institute of Health (NIH) and the U.S. Department of Energy. I bring this information forward because our future is bright. There will continue to be advances in figuring out the causes of human genetic diseases and disabilities.

<u>The Future and Creating Plans to Move Forward:</u>

The future will happen whether we are prepared for it or not. Planning and preparing for Aaron's future, both short-term and long-term, became my life's work. I would imagine and dream about what he would be like at the age of 5 or 10, but picturing my little boy at an older age was difficult, because I was stuck in the day-to-day activities of being a mother and raising our two children. We are parents. We want to see our children grow and thrive in life with a minimal number of negative experiences. I knew there would be social challenges for Aaron, but creating a plan gave me goals, hope, and a purpose to work toward with and for him.

It's difficult enough in "normal" situations to find time to spend hoping or dreaming about what could be. I realized early on that there was only so much I could hope or dream about. I had to be proactive. So mentally, as most humans do, I relied on what felt comfortable to me. We tend to draw upon what we are most familiar with—our family culture, personal experiences, how we were raised as children, the values we were taught, and how we were mentored to handle difficult life events. These experiences guided my thinking and decision-making abilities.

Digging deep into my mental files I used what worked for me in the past and discarded what didn't work. I trusted the knowledge, skills, and values cultivated by my past life experiences to take me forward into an uncertain future. Two wonderful parents who ran a loving home with age-appropriate expectations and teaching disciplines raised me. Everything I have come to know as a mother came from family relationships that made me feel safe, secure and nurtured. Growing up on a farm taught me about planning. We had to plan for each season of the year and understood that planning ahead would yield the best possible outcome.

As a young woman, choosing to become a professional registered nurse was a natural fit for me. Nurses anticipate change and plan for the unexpected, and their knowledge, practical skills, good values and planning ahead are requirements. On the farm, we nurtured the land, the crops and our livestock. That took critical thinking and care. The love of science, gaining knowledge, thinking critically, deeply caring for my patients and their families, listening to their life experiences and their personal goals all led me to be a well-rounded competent nurse.

Good fortune led me to a job at one of the leading health care providers in Chicago, caring for individuals who sustained spinal cord or traumatic brain injuries. Little did I know then that my deep understanding of neurology would one day help me understand how my own son's brain functioned.

Successfully raising Aaron required tapping into all of my life experiences, as well as learning every available fact about autism to positively affect Aaron's growth and development. I actively organized all of his therapies and worked with a team of experts in education. I maintained a journal of his progress and my thoughts, paying attention to what worked or did not work. This journal lived on the kitchen counter next to the coffee pot. Some mornings while having my coffee I would document his actions, behavior, speech, what caused his anxiety resulting in emotional meltdowns, and what gave him joy. These journal entries provided me with some of the tools necessary to assist him in achieving his goals.

We are all wired differently. Not every parent will have the same opportunity or the time to give their child that other parents might have. But the important goal is to always remember that your child with autism has one major tool at his or her disposal—You! So, you will do what needs to be done to the best of your ability. And that's what I hope I'll enable you to achieve as you read on by giving you the knowledge and the resources to meet your child's challenges.

CHAPTER 8

A is for ACCEPTANCE

Raising a child with a disability related to autism takes energy and determination. Facing challenging behaviors, or the simple difficulty of trying to communicate with your own child when you don't understand his language or the signs he is giving is exhausting.

Long before Aaron's official medical diagnosis in the autism spectrum, I knew and I had accepted that he marched to his own drumbeat. I don't know why things happen the way they do in life, but by chance one day I came across a greeting card with a quote by Henry David Thoreau that said:

> ***"If a man does not keep pace with his companions, perhaps it is because he hears a different drummer. Let him step to the music which he hears, however measured or far away."***

Aaron was just a baby, but I knew his brain processed his world to the beat of a different drummer. Aaron didn't like being held in my arms. He would arch his back as if he were in pain. He craved being bundled in a blanket. He cried and screamed when being placed in a crib. He found comfort and could sleep well in his car seat when we placed it on the floor. His eyes never looked at mine. Most of the time he looked just past my left shoulder. He did not engage with his surroundings much, and had little to no interest in exploring. Aaron did not like certain textures of clothing and screamed when placing shoes on his feet.

Just at the tail end of the recommended developmental time frame, however, Aaron managed to meet his developmental milestones. I became aware of small successes while physically working with him. I'd put him up on his hands and knees over a small beach ball working with his arms and legs to learn to crawl. All the while searching for more information and techniques to use with Aaron, I continued his normal physician follow-ups. He had various doctors who treated him for chronic ear infections or other common ailments, and I would explain what I found to be odd in Aaron's development. After many visits, one doctor said to me, *"I know you have a master's degree in neurology. I think you are looking too far into this and want something to be wrong with him."*

I felt shamed, as if I were being scolded. This professional was patronizing, and humiliated me. Later I learned about the term "refrigerator mothers." This now discredited mid to late 20th century theory by psychologist Dr. Bruno Bettelheim from the University of Chicago Orthogenic School claimed that autism was caused by the lack of a mother's love toward the child. Even though mothers denied it, the theory claimed that the mother had no control over it, and her child could sense the mother's deep-seated rejection when she herself could not sense it. Dr. Bettelheim's work became so popular after the publication of his book *"The empty fortress: Infantile autism and the birth of the self"*(1967), that he was featured on many programs including the 1960s popular Dick Cavett talk show. However, after being challenged by psychologist Bernard Rimland who had a son of his own with autism, Dr. Bettelheim's work was debunked. A fascinating documentary by David Simpson and J.J. Hanley (2002), explains how generations of women were branded as refrigerator mothers.

Physicians finally began to pay attention to the CDC at the turn of the 21st century, when the CDC initiated their campaign "First Signs," teaching professionals and the public about the first signs of autism. Prior to this autism movement, I continued trying everything that I could to advocate for Aaron's developmental needs early on, but the professionals wanted none of it. In the early 1990s, the signs of autism were not assessed.

It was demoralizing for me to be judged as a mother from others who knew nothing about my child or about me. If you research both "motherhood studies" and "disability studies" you'll see how society blamed mothers for their children's behavior leading to the term "mother-blame." (Zibricky, 2012) As important as establishing goals for Aaron's future became for me, I knew I had to do whatever I could to empower mothers and other family members by providing them with the tools necessary to minimize their struggles while attempting to help their child achieve the goals set for them.

No one knew Aaron like I did! I was his Mother! I observed Aaron as a baby and toddler, figured out his behavior and began to understand his communication methods, and adapted his environment accordingly so that he would be calmer. I just did not know how to help him. Then one day I went to a book store and again, by chance, I noticed a lonely book on a shelf with a title that spoke to me—"*The Child with Special Needs: Encouraging Intellectual and Emotional Growth*" by Stanley Greenspan and Serena Weider (1998). I later learned that the information provided in this book was quite popular. That's probably why there was only that one book on the shelf waiting for me.

Chapter 1 captured my attention immediately. It spoke about observing each child and noticing the subtle cues that were forms of communication. Much of what Greenspan and Weider investigated and wrote about reminded me of being a nurse, especially when it came to observing patients and noticing the subtleties with which they presented. I knew I could use their work to scaffold Aaron to his next developmental level and began by using the work of Greenspan and Weider and their approach called "Floortime." The technique of using **Floortime was exactly what it said it was—a matter of getting down on the floor with Aaron and doing my best to interact with him. The Floortime approach invited the child to adapt to and interact with their world.** This new technique would become part of the plan to promote Aaron's learning.

Play did not come naturally for him. I needed to observe and take his lead on what interested him. Using Floortime I found that it was not a set of rote learning techniques for other children in the autism spectrum. I learned that for Aaron, my observations of him, following his lead and then redirecting him as needed worked. By observing his body language and writing down what caused his anxiety, I discovered the patterns for things that would upset him and eventually began to predict his behavior. Adapting his environment to avoid him becoming upset helped me understand that he had no control on how his neurological system regulated itself.

It became my job to figure out how his mind processed information and then foster his strengths to learn and engage with others. I would sit with my legs crossed pretzel style on our large king-sized bed and place him in my body's makeshift chair. This position gave Aaron some nice deep pressure on his body that calmed him. Greenspan and Weider discussed the biological challenges of the sensory system in their book. I learned about the continuous biological feedback that the sensory system must interpret to react to on a constant basis. It wasn't until a few years later that I learned about how autism and the sensory system are interconnected.

When Aaron was 3 years old, he entered early childhood education provided by the local school district. His teacher gave me a Xeroxed article from one of her professional journals on a new theory called "sensory integration" (SI). She didn't know much about it but said it sounded like something that would help Aaron. I went to our local library to use their Internet and search engines because they had access to research journals and found other articles about sensory integration. These were shared with his teacher and his occupational therapist. Most of the literature came from the work of occupational therapist and educational psychologist Dr. A. Jean Ayers. She studied the way the brain organizes itself and how it processes sensory information. In the 1990s, little was known about sensory processing in the brain or about Dr. Ayers' work on sensory integration theory. Many professionals from various fields didn't take her sensory integration theory seriously. Today, however, sensory integration is a common term, and a universal therapy when working with students diagnosed in the autism spectrum or other disabilities.

I learned as much as I could about SI therapy on my own, and adapted our house to help Aaron's neurological system by either calming it down or making him more alert using SI therapeutic items that I made myself. I sewed weighted blankets, weighted wrist, arm and vest clothing. In the basement I used a plastic kiddie pool filled with beans to pour on his body (dressed in shorts) for stimulation. Other items such as a beanbag chair or swing in the basement provided the sensory stimulation that he needed. None of the therapies were done without an educated occupational therapist who was also learning about SI. Together we accessed information on SI and adapted both our home and the school to help Aaron learn.

It's important for every parent to know that after decades of research, sensory processing theory and sensory integration therapy has gained its credible reputation. Sensory Integration is now a common household term and **SI therapy has become a fundamental part of an educational program for children with disabilities. I would strongly recommend working with a professional occupational therapist at the school or privately to assess best practices in SI therapy, come up with a plan, and measure the progress.**

CHAPTER 9

M is for MAKING ACTION PLANS (MAPs)

I managed Aaron's development from the time he was born, meaning that I documented everything, tried interventions that I thought would work and collaborated with professionals in the educational system. As Aaron grew and progressed, I became more motivated to learn about autism, the newest findings on this disorder, and evidence-based therapies, deciding which of those therapies might benefit him. Most therapies required expensive specialists not covered by insurance plans. I knew of parents in the 1990s who would spend anywhere from $50,000 to $90,000 dollars a year on one type of therapy. I also knew that we could not afford this, so again I relied upon my determination to keep moving forward.

I first learned the term "Person-Centered Planning" when Aaron was in kindergarten. **Person-Centered Planning (PCP) is a process-oriented approach focusing on the needs of people with disabilities and their families by providing direction for their lives, not on the systems that may or may not be available to serve them.**

An education grant funded by the State of Illinois Board of Education, titled the "Illinois Autism/Pervasive Developmental Disorder Training and Technical Assistance Project" began in 2002 by creating numerous teams throughout the State as a "trainer-of-trainers" model. Ten teams of five people each were trained as leaders to train others in the Illinois school system, **with one parent required on each team.** I was one of those parent team members, and over the course of five years I trained many people about the most current evidence available on the autism spectrum and the most innovative therapies used. My introduction to PCP through that Illinois grant focused on a basic planning process called Making Action Plans (MAPs). During the hands-on 5-day trainings, parents on the training teams could create a plan to assist them in generating a vision for the futures of their children. Today that program receives minimal funding from the Illinois Department of Human Services Bureau of Early Intervention (2018), however it remains current in its evidence and is a strong and valuable resource for education professionals and parents.

A MAP is an action plan requiring participation from others and is probably one of the most valuable tools a family can utilize. The individual with the disability is at the center of the plan, and the MAP focuses on their wants, their dreams, and their hopes. There may be advocates for the individual, but when possible the lead voice IS the individual—what they want their future to be. The individual comes away knowing that his or her thoughts and ideas about their own future are important and are to be honored.

As the acronym suggests, a MAP maps out—provides direction—as to where the person with a disability wants to go and/or what outcomes they want to achieve. The process requires people to develop creative opportunities and an action plan to work toward accomplishing the hopes and dreams of the individual.

In order to make the MAP process most successful, the gifts, strengths, and talents of the person with the disability must be highlighted. Maximizing these positives provides support for the dreams of the person who is the focus of the plan, and sends the individual with a disability the message that their thoughts about the future are important and honored. Since the desired outcomes have a personal meaning to the individual with the disability, it fosters the approach that those outcomes will be achieved.

When Aaron finished second grade, he made it clear to his teachers, and to Greg and I, that he didn't want to stay in a self-contained classroom for students with disabilities. He was being bused 45 minutes away from home into another school district. He wasn't happy and wasn't meeting his goals. He felt out of place, controlled and wanted to be with the kids he was growing up with and playing ball with in his driveway. So Greg and I asked the educational team what Aaron could do in the future and how we could focus on being positive and supportive of his goals. We wanted to respond to Aaron's wish to be mainstreamed, if at all possible. This required a big shift in attitude and new thinking in education. So based on what I had learned in the statewide training, Aaron, Greg and I invited the educational team to join us as a family for a MAPs process.

About 15-20 people attended Aaron's first Map in our living room—family members, neighborhood friends, teachers, school administrator, church minister and state service coordinators. Goals with completion dates were created and people were asked to be on board to assist in making the goals happen. The teachers and administrator were curious, excited and apprehensive as to how this would work as they were legally bound to write measureable learning goals.

A requirement of a MAP is to have a facilitator guide the group, and an illustrator record the conversation by drawing or listing out on a poster what the individual and group discussed. The objective was to keep the process simple with some step-by-step procedures to focus the group on what is positive and possible.

Each MAP process had basic questions that included:

1. **The history of the person with the disability. (See Fig. 1)**
2. **What is their dream and where do they see themselves? (See Fig. 2)**
3. **What are the "nightmares" (things to avoid)? (See Fig. 3)**
4. **Who is the person? Or, "how would you describe yourself, or how do others describe you?" (See Fig. 4)**
5. **What are the person's gifts, strengths and talents? (See Fig. 5)**
6. **What is the plan of action? (See Fig. 6)**

To give you a better idea of what occurred, I've included the following MAP to show and explain how the process worked. Although it might seem daunting at first, it's well worth the time, effort and work. Both Greg and I attribute much of Aaron's success to these sessions. Aaron's 17-year use of MAPs will be summarized at the end of this Chapter.

The process of doing a MAP begins with covering the person's history.

FIGURE 1

What is Aaron's History?

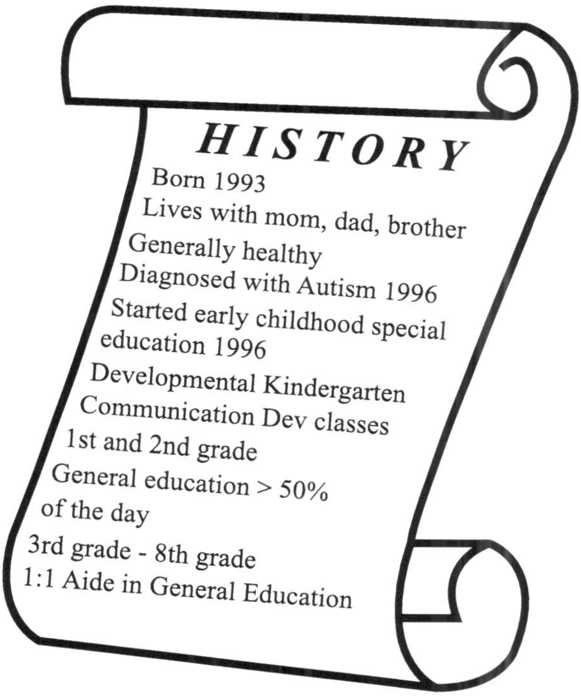

From this illustration, Aaron's history included being born in 1993, living with his parents and brother and being generally healthy. It recorded that he was diagnosed with autism in 1996, started early childhood special education, and went to developmental kindergarten and a communication development classroom for 1st and 2nd grades. This history ends noting that Aaron was in general education with typical peers more than 50% of his day from 3rd grade until 8th grade and required a 1:1 classroom aide to help him with his work.

FIGURE 2

What is the Dream?

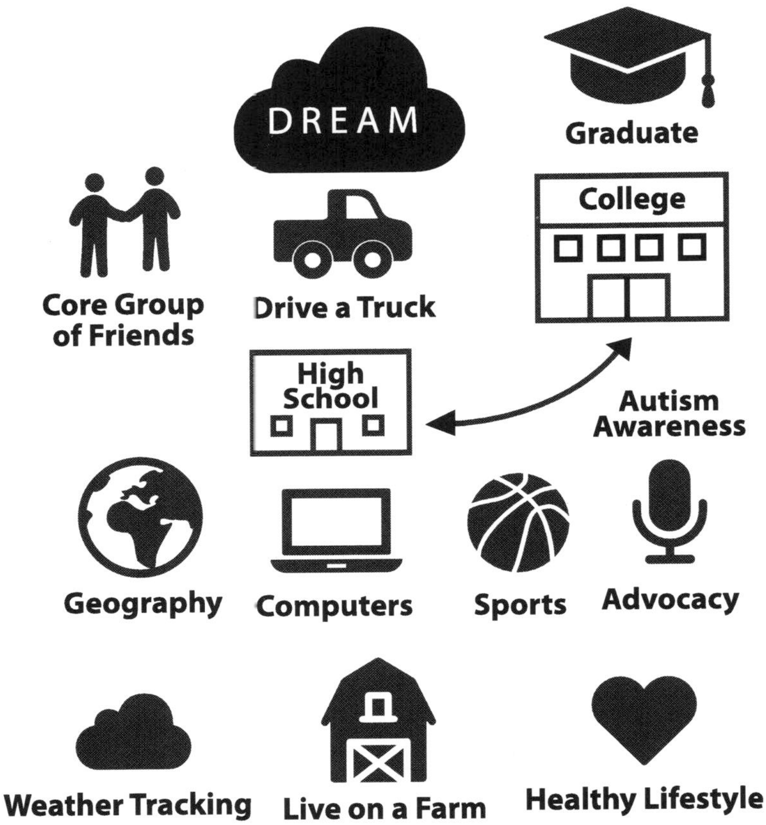

Aaron's expressed his dream to graduate from high school and go to college. He wanted to have a core group of friends, drive a red truck, work with maps and geography, use computers, participate in sports, be an autism advocate, learn about the weather, live on a farm and have a healthy lifestyle.

FIGURE 3

What did Aaron want to avoid? What was the "nightmare?"

Aaron explained that his nightmare would be not to graduate from high school when his friends would graduate at age 18. He was tired of being bullied by some students and afraid of being isolated and left alone. Aaron also expressed that he felt his educational goals were set too low for him. He wanted his teachers to have higher expectations and believe that he could meet his goals both educationally and socially. Aaron also felt that no one would listen to what he felt he needed to succeed in life. He did not want to work in a fast-paced environment such as McDonalds. And finally he was worried that he would not know how to advocate for himself leading to him being excluded socially.

FIGURE 4

Who is the Person? Who is Aaron?

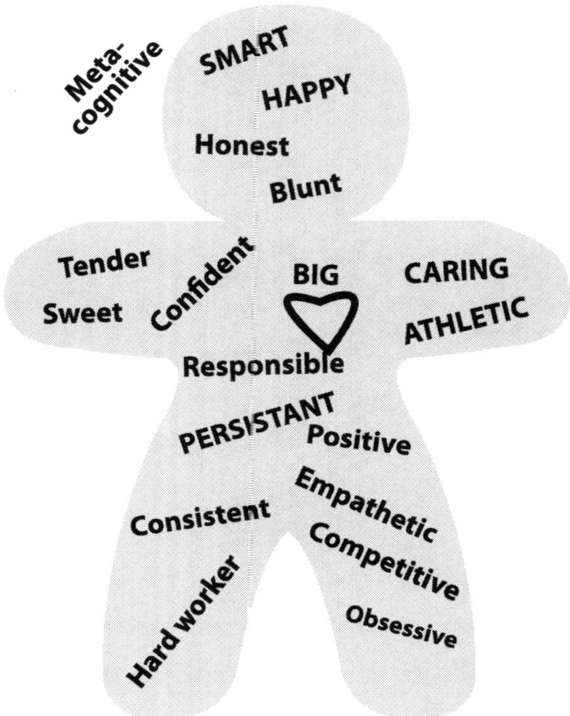

During the MAP process in our home, the attendees described their impressions of Aaron, aware that the MAP focuses on the positive. This importance of this exercise for Aaron cannot be emphasized enough. People were honest. They presented his personality with solid feedback. They described Aaron as having a metacognition, meaning that he had an awareness of and understanding of his own thoughts. Family, friends, teachers, an administrator, and our minister identified that he was smart, happy, honest, blunt, tender, sweet, confident, having a big heart, caring, responsible, persistent, positive, consistent, empathetic, a hard worker, competitive and obsessive.

FIGURE 5

Gifts, Strengths, Talents

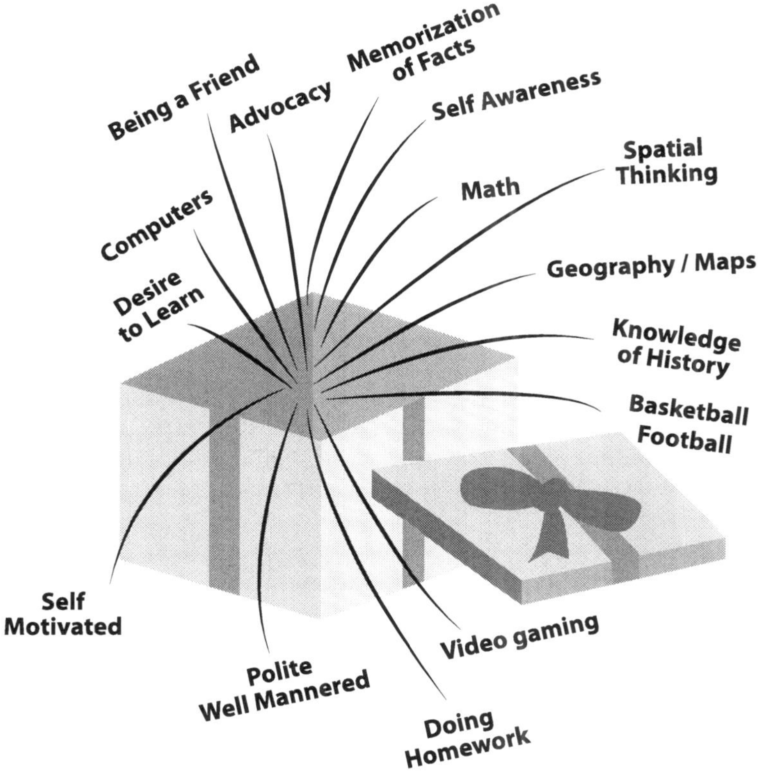

The MAP identified that Aaron possessed many gifts, strengths and talents. These positive attributes would be used to facilitate the dream. In summary, Aaron was seen as being a good friend, with the gifted ability to memorize many facts about various topics including history and sports. He could also memorize geographical areas and maps. But his talent came through when it came to having spatial awareness, meaning that he could interpret where we were going without ever looking at a physical map. He was described as being excellent with computers, self-motivated, polite and doing his work well.

FIGURE 6

Plan of Action

GOALS	ASSISTANCE
Continue with clubs, and sports	Parents, Coaches, IEP Team
Advocacy	Parents, IEP Team Advocacy Groups
Transportation Drivers Education	IEP Team, Parents Family Members
IEP Goals for Advocacy Social Skills	IEP Team, Parents
Transition Goals for College: Writing, reading, technology, ADA	IEP Team, Parents, Advocacy Groups
Socialization: Dances, Dating, Recreation	Friends, Parents
Household Skills	Parents, Family
Finances	Parents, Family, IEP Team
Routine Appts: Doctor, Dentist, Pharmacy, Psychologist	Parents

Learning about MAPs helped me understand that Aaron, Greg and I would need help in planning Aaron's future. Having MAPs as an ongoing process, the emotional and physical strength and endurance to commit ourselves to seeing this process through began with getting people on board—our family members, family friends, Aaron's friends, neighbors, professionals and people who saw Aaron on a regular basis including the minister of our church.

Over the course of 17 years, our family has conducted four MAPs. The original MAP illustrated above was the largest. We eventually scaled back to inviting two or three people whom Aaron wanted to work with on subsequent MAPs. The second MAP was when Aaron was in 5th grade to start preparing for junior high.

As a Mom, I always planned ahead. My farming background taught me that important lesson. So, I believed that waiting to plan for junior high while in 7th grade was too late. The rule of thumb for me was to plan 1-2 years ahead. Planning for transitioning to a large community high school of 2300 students with over 66 clubs to choose from got me to thinking about all the opportunities that Aaron could maximize. It became essential for Aaron to plan for what HE wanted. The MAP process helped us plan. The last formal MAP took place when Aaron was a junior in high school when traditional transition planning by federal law is required. We focused on what Aaron would be capable of to meet his goal of going to college.

Drawing upon the gifts, strengths and talents of individuals with ASD is essential when picking a college major and/or planning for careers. The incredible talent of spatial thinking, the extraordinary navigation of computers and the amazing ability to memorize geographical maps and historical data led to a major in Geography and a minor in Geographic Information Systems (GIS). The possibility of internship programs that are part of the GIS curriculum could include working in the areas of agriculture or in rural communities.

Many outcomes from Aaron's previous actions were met. For example, participating on the high school football team led to the social skills needed to join a campus fraternity. Aaron's past experiences of speaking about autism both locally and nationally resulted in the entire fraternity taking on local community outreach programs working with children with autism. Speaking engagements also led to the first Autism Speaks (Autism Speaks U, 2014) group on campus. In addition, learning independent living skills identified in the dream promoted living on campus in a dorm with a future goal of having an apartment with friends. Aaron's claim of "I want to go to college' was possible after all. He has graduated and is working for a local Village in their G.I.S. program.

Overall, there are no set chronological times when a MAP should be done. As a family, we recommend using the MAPs process when there are transitions into various educational settings or major life events such as now as Aaron prepares to live on his own.

CHAPTER 10

I is for INFORMATION

When your child is diagnosed with autism, the reality doesn't hit immediately. Shock settles in first, followed by denial, and then the reality. For me, the words of that doctor who diagnosed Aaron rang through my head. *He will never know you as his Mother. He will never live on his own.* Once I became aware of the hard work in front of Greg and I, understanding the importance of persistence in viewing Aaron's gifts and strengths and talents became imperative! So I just worked and hoped, constantly aware that my education as his mother would enable him as our toddler became a child, an adolescent, a college student, and a 25-year old man.

How did we come to this place in Aaron's life? Information! We flooded ourselves with Information! So much change has taken place since that diagnosis all those years ago, not just in how the autism spectrum disorder is viewed, but also in how educators view students with autism.

Looking back, I couldn't even begin to imagine what Aaron's future would be like had it not been for the information we obtained and the education he received. The realization that there wasn't even a law in the United States to protect individuals with disabilities is inconceivable! Legal changes didn't come about until 1975 during the Civil Rights Movement. A lot of different groups piggybacked themselves onto the Civil Rights Movement, including people with disabilities.

The Education of Handicapped Children Act (later renamed the Individuals With Disabilities Education Act, or IDEA) became law in 1975. What is particularly interesting about this is that parents didn't know—were never told—that their child was in "Special Education" or that they even had any learning problems prior to this time. It wasn't until around the Civil Rights Movement that parents became more aware and began asking, *"My child was placed in special education? My child received special help?"* It was an astonishing awareness for many.

The law was reportedly changed because a parent sued her school district for not informing her of her child's placement in "special class." The case went to the U.S. Supreme Court and resulted in the passage of IDEA.

The first President Bush signed IDEA into law and it became part of the Americans with Disabilities Act; however, IDEA was just for individuals in public schools. In 2004 IDEA was reauthorized to become the Education Improvement Act.

Many changes have since been made to assure that children with disabilities receive a "free and appropriate public education." It is free in the public school system and is paid for by tax dollars. The word "appropriate" is especially important as it means that an educational team determines whether the education is appropriate to the individual student. For example, if you have a child with Down's syndrome and the parents want their child to take tennis lessons, the school will not pay for that because it is not appropriate.

It's also important to know that IDEA recognizes thirteen disabilities that qualify someone for special education. The qualification begins at the age of 3. There are usually communities that do a "child find." A newspaper may carry an advertisement for "child find" and you can take your child who hasn't yet started kindergarten to the school district to see whether they qualify for special education.

If a child is diagnosed with any type of disability before age 3 (starting at the age of 1) they are covered through Child and Family Connections (CFC). CFC will begin working with a baby right away by providing occupational therapy, speech therapy, and any area where the child is falling behind. Once they reach their 3rd birthday they no longer qualify for that assistance. They are tested again and at that point the school district picks up taxpayer dollars for special education. They can then utilize the expertise of speech therapists, occupational therapists, nurses and other different services. That law extends until the age of 21. At the individual's 22nd birthday they stop qualifying for public education. That is a huge change, and is why I want to discuss this and encourage you to BE AWARE of the Federal laws and your individual State laws.

The laws vary according to age and the State in which the individual lives. All of the previous information relates to Federal laws, but it is known that States can always do more, but never less than Federal laws. For example, in some States students qualify for special education until they are 26 years of age, thereby allowing them to override Federal law. The cutoff age for Illinois for public education services is the 22nd birthday.

A huge question for parents is what happens at the 22nd (or other cutoff) birthday, as the services end abruptly. That is where advance planning comes in, and where the MAP plays such an important role. Typically schools are required by law to start with what they call a "transition plan" at the age of 14, while some schools start at 16 years of age. You have to learn what the Federal law says and understand that, by law, the schools have to begin transition planning because going from IDEA into the American with Disabilities Act (ADA) is like jumping off of a cliff without wings.

I can't imagine not having a MAP plan, or Aaron just being thrust into adulthood while we're wondering, *"OK, now what? We don't know what we're supposed to do now."* **It's critical to know the laws and start early** to start thinking about where the individual, or a person advocating for them wants to be.

With regard to the Americans with Disabilities Act (also known as the ADA throughout the United States), people who need accommodations with a wheelchair, or assistance getting on and off an airplane, qualify for the ADA. **The most important thing to know here is to look for "reasonable accommodations."** When Greg, Aaron and I worked with the school system they provided "free and appropriate" public education. Now working under the ADA, they provide "reasonable accommodation." So, as an adult, Aaron has a job and he receives reasonable accommodations for his autism.

Aaron had to be prepared for this change—for going from the IDEA to the ADA—and we, as parents, had to prepare ourselves as well. It was a difficult adjustment. When he graduated high school he no longer qualified under IDEA because he graduated. He was now in an adult world because he chose to be—he chose to graduate from high school. There were no additional IDEA services available to him in an educational setting. He decided he wanted to go to college; however, it would have to be under a new law—the ADA.

Looking back at Aaron's illustration, part of his "dream" was a four-year college, and it was a dream going back to when he was a young boy. I'll never forget when he exclaimed at one point, "I'm going to college." Shock! Yes, I wanted to remain positive, but I also had to remind myself of his skills. So I focused on his gifts, his strengths, and his talents, which we discovered and developed as part of his MAP. We focused on his qualities, asking ourselves how they would fit in various scenarios.

For example, in one college course on setting up electrical circuits, he could just look at the sheet of paper and figure it out without using the math they encouraged him to use. He could see it spatially. He also had an uncanny ability to recall all the trips we took years earlier and how to get back to those same places. He'd say to me, "Mom, everybody calls me a human GPS." Because of that I learned to understand that spatial awareness is a unique gift, highly related to memory. The question now was how to pull out those extraordinary talents so others could see what Aaron was capable of doing.

Prior to Aaron's graduating high school, I didn't think he could do college level work because upon graduation at age 18 he was writing three paragraphs, where most people were writing five pages or more. Three paragraphs were not going to get him into college and certainly were not going to get him a degree from college. But he was insistent, and "persistent," as was once brought up in a MAP session. Also, Aaron doesn't forget. He remembers everything. So he told me, "I can do this Mom. If I have to learn how to write more sentences, then I'll learn how to write more sentences." He had the basics. He could write a theme sentence and would have support sentences in his paragraph, and also could do really good transition sentences.

Because he never wavered in his wish to go to college, we sought out our local junior college. They wanted to put him into automotive classes and enroll him in skilled vocational training. Aaron didn't want that. He said, "No, I want to take classes." The school said he would not be able to qualify for 100-level courses, and 100-level courses meant you earn college credit. So he was not at the level to earn college credit. Courses beginning with zero did not earn college credit, but that's where Aaron began and he learned to write. He told people at disability services under the ADA that he was going to learn to write. Aaron also has OCD (obsessive-compulsive disorder) and has always been like that. Aaron made it a point to tell the junior college instructor that he was going to learn to write a five-page paper within a year. I chuckled because I knew it was a tall order. He did it! He learned to write five pages, stick to the topic, with every single paragraph perfectly written. He had assistive technology, which meant that he would talk the paper because writing for him was hard. So Aaron spoke into a microphone, dictated the whole essay and then someone (who was part of a "reasonable accommodation" of the ADA) wrote it out for him.

The next year of Aaron's junior college experience he took 100-level courses and insisted to Greg and I that he would apply to a four-year institution. We went back to the MAP and looked at institutions with majors and minors that would match his strengths. He chose Geography as a major at a small liberal arts college, and minored in Geo-Spatial Information Systems—GIS. He never had to take the A.C.T. because he did well at a junior college. He was accepted at a four-year institution without taking the A.C.T.

None of this could have been accomplished without our seeking out more Information. Agencies will not come looking for you—you have to search them out and be persistent in your follow-up. Don't assume there is no answer for your child—just keep digging until you are satisfied. Your child is worth all the time it takes.

Aaron's involvement with GIS involves gathering data, creating a computer program and placing the data in that program. He explains it as, "Anything you want to put on a map, I can create that map and I can put all the data on the map." Right now he is working at a local village hall and does their entire mapping. If they need something in transportation, or a parking lot looked at, or checking on the curbing system and it can be placed on a map, that is Aaron's responsibility.

While in college, he mapped out all the Veteran's Administrations in the Chicagoland area to see where veterans could go to receive health care. He chose a particular population (veterans) and had to trace and find all the various types of transportation methods—whether bus, Uber, trains—and map it all out, then direct it to all the Veteran's Administrations in the Chicagoland area. He did it flawlessly and got a great grade. I had no clue what he was doing, but he saw it because of his gift of spatial awareness.

He also expressed an interest in tectonic plates. I knew nothing about tectonic plates, but he explained that they are under the ocean and move because of the intense heat in the Earth's core and they make up the surface of the earth. He did a global collection of data on how fast those plates are moving and how it relates to the occurrence of earthquakes.

Finally, in senior year, he became obsessed with 9/11 because of the many people with disabilities who died in the Towers simply because they could not get out—there was no evacuation plan for a catastrophe of that proportion. He was so upset by the fact that there were people in wheelchairs, and there were no working elevators since the Towers were on fire, and that those with disabilities died because no one could get to them. It struck Aaron that people with disabilities perished and their friends died because there wasn't an escape plan, so he decided that his college had to have an escape plan in every single campus building, which was huge. Much to his surprise, most buildings had escape plans, but not all of them. So he went in, assessed and collected data, physically walked through every single building and interviewed people with disabilities who lived in various dorms. Places like the Library where people would have to be carried down stairs, or inaccessible bathrooms needed to be addressed. He identified the areas in the College that needed a change and this became his Capstone project.

Finally, he had to pass his exams on his own. He qualified for what was "reasonable" and a reasonable accommodation was someone who would read his exams to him. His professors were outstanding and realized how he would make a difference in the world. They were willing to work with him. That's part of the MAP—working with people who honestly understand that people with disabilities are more than capable of doing well. It was a really good experience for Aaron.

After graduation, we worked with Aaron to enhance his interviewing skills, which were not very strong. Someone informed us that our village was going to spend money to hire a consultant to do their GIS work and input the data for various projects. Aaron interviewed and when asked if he could do that he said yes, and listed five types of computer programs he could use. They were surprised by his ability to use all those programs and from that point on he has had a full-time job with benefits at our local village.

Key for people with disabilities is to possess a full time job and qualifying for obtaining insurance. So many people are held back because they don't have insurance and somehow have to qualify for Medicaid. Aaron is now on Medicaid, and a lot of his friends from college who have many gifts and skills and talents are on Medicaid because they weren't able to complete the requirement of the college. It's heartbreaking when we live in a world where individuals are more than capable of doing the work, but they are not able to get insurance.

Looking back to that first MAP session for our 8-year old son, I would never have believed how far he would come. Having the proper Information at our disposal throughout Aaron's school years and knowing what he was eligible for in terms of programs for individuals with disabilities was essential. The value of working with the support of family, friends, and educators in the MAP sessions to build Aaron's future based on his desires cannot be diminished. Learning to imagine a positive future for someone who was nonverbal at the age of 3-1/2 and accompany him on his life's journey has been extraordinary.

So, if you can believe in "positive" and "possible" and you start working early toward "the Dream," it will happen.

CHAPTER 11

L is for LEADERSHIP

Greg and I are so fortunate to have a son who has exhibited a number of leadership skills over the years, which we might not have thought were possible when his diagnosis was first made at age three. Throughout this journey, doubting that Aaron's future would meet the dreams he had established as part of his MAP sessions became one of the more difficult problems we had to conquer. Sometimes we forgot to trust Aaron's tenacity because we couldn't always see the whole picture. Aaron conquered our "doubting" problem for us, by his persistence and his belief in himself, and by consistently showing us that he could be his own advocate.

Aaron has always been expressively open and strong-minded about what he wanted to do and as his parents, it was critical for us to know his ambitions and seek out resources to make those ambitions Aaron's reality. When Aaron decided to be on the high school football team, he could barely throw a football and understanding abstract strategic plays could have quashed his dream. But he insisted he could do this, so Greg worked with the football coach and eventually Aaron not only became part of the team, but formed strong friendships with his fellow players. Those friendships remain today, a testimony to Aaron's sense of loyalty.

Another obstacle of sorts made itself known when Aaron decided that he was ready to get a driver's license. Once he made up his mind on a thing, he became relentless So we met with the driver's education staff, and even hired a private driving instructor to get Aaron through the lessons and eventually his driver's test. He received his driver's license at age 18, another skill toward independent living conquered.

On a few occasions, Aaron accompanied Greg and I on speaking engagements locally and nationally on the subject of raising a child with autism and planning for their future. He walked on stage, spoke about who he was and how autism did not define him. He was in control and confident.

Aaron's decision to enter a four-year college was probably the biggest shocker of all for Greg and I. We were aware of his writing and reading limitations and realized that those issues could well be what finally stopped

Aaron's pursuit of college. Instead, Aaron learned that he had to be able to write an acceptable paper of more than three paragraphs if he was to be accepted, so he knuckled down at a junior college taking non-credit courses in writing. Two years later he could write a five-page theme paper, and applied to a small college that had excellent supporting programs for students with disabilities.

These are just a few of the examples of Aaron's strong personality, his sense of confidence and his refusal to give up without a fight. Each of these traits is an element of a leadership personality. Over the course of the four MAP sessions conducted with friends, colleagues, educators, and family members, they described Aaron as possessing leadership traits. Among them: metacognition, honesty, confidence, caring, responsibility, persistence, consistency, empathy, hardworking, competitive, loyal, self-motivated, and more. His experience as a football team member developed his social skills and enabled him to participate as a member of a fraternity while in college. His awareness of the needs of others resulted in performing a study of his college campus to assure the safety of disabled students. His confidence in advocating for autism encouraged the participation of his fraternity in an Autism Awareness program on campus. Aaron's leadership skills have shown themselves over and over again.

Many studies have been done on leadership qualities of young people and adults, but not many have focused on developing leaders among young people with disabilities. It is important for parents to recognize how important it is for their child with a disability to develop these skills.

The Waisman Center at the University of Wisconsin in Madison has an excellent website devoted to encouraging leadership skills for individuals with developmental disabilities. The program is the University Center for Excellence in Developmental Disabilities. The following is a list of their "Tips for Youth," which is a valuable tool. I encourage all parents to share this list with their child. More information on programs for students with developmental disabilities can be found at their website:

www.waismanucedd.wiscweb.wisc.edu

1. Believe that you can accomplish anything. Set goals for what you want to do and make a plan to achieve those goals.
2. Connect with the faculty and staff (e.g. teachers, guidance counselors, support staff, case managers) and draw on them as resources for leadership and volunteer opportunities.
3. Find a mentor. Seek out someone you can completely confide in who will support you in the development of your leadership skills.
4. Be a mentor to younger students with disabilities. Help them to develop their leadership skills by sharing your experiences and connecting them with available opportunities.
5. Participate in youth leadership conferences. Take advantage of leadership workshops that involve both youth and parents, since parents can be a valuable resource for supporting leadership skills. Help organize conferences and other youth leadership projects.
6. Create a peer support network. Connect with other youth leaders with disabilities, including those in different communities. You can share experiences (what you did, what worked for you, etc.) and learn from one another. Form a council of older youth with disabilities to serve as a resource for younger youth with disabilities.
7. Get involved and take every opportunity possible. Join after-school activities such as clubs or sports. Find an area of skill you'd like to develop where you can gain confidence. Have organizations you are involved in partner with other organizations when development youth leadership activities.
8. Get involved in leadership activities early in your educational career. Start small. Start at your school by joining a committee or an extracurricular club, and then branch out to other networks.
9. Attend summer camps. Camps often build leadership and team building into their activities and objectives. Attending camps also allows you to get away from home and develop independence in a structured environment. Most camps provide great opportunities to enhance your leadership skills.
10. Take challenging classes in high school and college. Do not limit your academic opportunities. Request the modifications and supports necessary to succeed in these classes.

11. Become active in the local disability community and connect with other leaders. Go to your neighborhood center for leadership opportunities and share these with other youth.
12. Take advantage of speaking on panels or in front of large groups at school. These are good opportunities to practice communication and public speaking skills.
13. Take initiative to be independent. For example, sit at a different lunch table to meet new people or call your friends to do something instead of waiting for them to call you.
14. Be assertive. Make sure people know what accommodations you need and what you don't need. Help parents and adults understand your needs, and be patient when they don't understand. Don't be afraid to ask for help.
15. Assume responsibility for taking the steps needed to achieve your goals to become a leader.
16. Being a leader doesn't mean doing all of the work or being in the limelight, but rather working together on a team to accomplish a shared goal.
17. Participate in and lead your own IEP meeting. This is a great way to practice many different types of leadership skills (e.g. communication, self-advocacy, decision-making).
18. Know what situations you are getting into and what the expectations are. For example, if you are going to take a new class, obtain the syllabus or meet with the teacher prior to beginning the class.
19. Be a self-advocate. Speak up for yourself, what you believe in, and what you need to participate fully in, both in school and the community.
20. Be yourself and love yourself for who you are. Share your disability with others.
21. Be creative. Do not let other people define what you can or cannot do. Being a leader and working with/around your disability sometimes involves thinking outside of the box.

CHAPTER 12

Y is for YARANNA

Yaranna means Friendships. This is the word that highlights the important part of Aaron's life—his friendships and his family. It is an Urdu word used in the language of India. I cannot think of a more fitting way to end this discussion than to talk about Aaron's friends, and to talk about Greg's and my families.

Yaranna—Friendships—have helped us believe in Aaron and have guided him. During our first MAP held at our home about twenty years ago, Aaron had a few of his school friends there to participate. Amazingly, much like Geography and GIS, we worked hard at relationships and these same people who were present at the MAP when Aaron was eight years old are still his friends today—his best friends, and I bring this out because this happened all because of a third grade teacher.

Third grade was the first time Aaron was in regular education. He had been in Special Ed until then. Although Greg and I worked closely with the school district, they told us that he was not ready for regular education, and that he didn't have the skill set. They showed us all of his testing, indicating he was a few years behind peers of his age. Aaron kept insisting. "I can be with everybody else. I want to be with everybody else." Greg and I finally just asked the school, "Please, just give us a chance. Just give Aaron a chance."

What made the difference was his third grade teacher. She had been instrumental in developing what Aaron "could" be. She worked with Aaron. It was interesting that she would take his writings and make them into maps. She knew he loved maps, so here we go with another key piece from his third grade teacher. He struggled, but she knew how to tap in. She knew he was smart. But she just knew that he learned differently and that was ok.

I approached his third grade teacher and I said to her, "Are there any boys in the class that say 'hi' to Aaron, or who hang out with Aaron?" She said, "Yes, there are two boys that do." And I asked, "Do you think that maybe I could meet their mothers, that we could get together some time?" She responded that she thought she could arrange that. So I was introduced to these two mothers and their sons, and I complimented the mothers on how wonderful their sons were.

I explained that Aaron had autism and he would struggle with some of his behaviors, he would struggle with reading and writing, and I was wondering whether our boys could get together some time over a weekend. The one mother replied, "Sure, we can do that." The boys were on board with it. They said, "Yeah, we like Aaron. Yeah, we can do that." And I can't ever thank them enough, because just this past weekend they were all up at the bar during the Chicago Bears game.

These young men, together with Aaron, have been friends now for more than 17 years. They are together most weekends. They go camping, they go hiking, and they go on vacations. One of them plays in a band, so Aaron became the band manager and cares for all the equipment. The other guys sing and play drums and perform gigs out at bars in a local town. So Aaron has had a really full set of Yaranna—a full set of Friendships.

Now when I look back and reflect on his first MAP I think, "Oh my gosh there it is." He talked about having a core group of friends—it's right there under "the dream." The "nightmare" was that he would be alone, he'd be isolated and he didn't want that—and he didn't get that.

Also in the nightmare it showed "setting the bar too low." You are only going to go as high as the expectations you put upon yourself and the expectations your teachers put on you. Aaron just said, "don't set the bar too low for me." Greg and I never did, his college professors certainly didn't and the junior college and high school didn't either. Aaron has always had the bar raised a little higher so he could be successful. When I look back at the nightmare and I picture him sitting at the isolation table all by himself, I realize we avoided that nightmare. Aaron has a full range of friends from high school, from the fraternity brothers at his small college who he keeps in contact with, and from the professors with whom he's maintained contact. He sees them as good friends, and I think they are very proud of Aaron because they saw how hard he worked to succeed.

Aaron has developed well in life. He continues to impress us. He continues to surprise us, and he's always coming out with "I want to do this." Lately—last year to be exact—because college was over and he wanted to find something new, Aaron looked into Taekwondo at the suggestion of a friend of mine. Responding to that competitive side of his personality he decided to pursue Taekwondo and to become a black belt. It's taken him almost a year and a half, but he is now a black belt in Taekwondo and he working toward achieving the various steps upward to go beyond the black belt.

Aaron's first friends, and all of our family members who supported us have made Aaron's dream possible. So again, **if you can believe in "positive" and "possible" and you start working early toward "the Dream," it WILL happen.**

ONWARD

IN CLOSING

Dear Aaron:

As you know, our promise to you has always been "Nothing About Me Without Me," meaning that everything written or shared from our private lives has been OK'd for disclosure by all of us, and that includes everything written in this book by Dad and me.

Whenever an opportunity came our way we seized the moment, hoping that by chance it would be a positive opportunity for you. Aaron, you've taken many chances. You are a testament to taking chances, never giving up and always advocating for what you wanted for yourself. Early on, when you were only about eight years old, you were described as being confident, persistent, and a hard worker. That reminds me of our favorite song, Chances, by Five for Fighting, which was the end-title song in the 2009 movie The Blind Side. You and I saw that film together. It was based on the true story about the success of professional football player Michael Oher. The themes of taking chances, having love and support, working hard for success and believing in yourself helped make your dreams become a reality.

You are the inspiration for these chapters, Aaron. Thank you for allowing Dad and I to share them.

Love,

Mom

ACKNOWLEDGEMENTS

The acknowledgements at the beginning of this book represent those who walked the journey with Greg and I from the beginning. Their contributions can never be diminished.

Having tools such as Person-Centered Planning and Making Action Plans (MAPs) helped us navigate the way to life-long success for Aaron. Thanks to the Illinois State Board of Education, the Illinois Autism-Pervasive Developmental Disorder Training and Technical Assistance Project, and our local school district for giving me the opportunity to become a trainer for others in the State. It opened many doors for students with autism, their families, educational professionals and the wider community by teaching how planning for the future is a fundamental necessity when raising a child in the autism spectrum. Thank you to all the parents and professionals I've had the privilege of working with over these past 22 years.

As I took the lead on Aaron's education, Greg took the lead on the financial planning. We each navigated our areas of expertise and shared our experiences with others. We're so proud of our sons, Aaron and his younger sibling Ben, for being extraordinary young men who have worked hard toward making their life dreams become their realities.

Finally, thanks to my husband Greg for inviting me to be a part of this second edition of F.A.M.I.L.Y. He worked long and hard on the original book. His decision to include the educational/social development aspect of Aaron's growth wasn't made lightly. The result provides a comprehensive look at what it takes to raise a child with autism, and in particular, how that process requires the commitment of the entire family. So, Greg, thank you for allowing me to share my recollections with yours in this revised edition of F.A.M.I.L.Y. I'm honored to be a part of this worthwhile project.

PROVIDE CARE JOURNAL

For:____

LIVE, WORK, PLAY, WORSHIP

Date:____

LIVE

Family Information

LIVE

Daily Routine

LIVE

Medications

LIVE

Dietary Restrictions

LIVE

Food Likes and Dislikes

LIVE

Living Arrangements

LIVE

Other

WORK

Employer

WORK

Employer

WORK

Manager/Team Leader

WORK

Detailed Work Skills

WORK

Future Employment Opportunities

WORK

Limitations

WORK

Continuing Education

WORK

Other

PLAY

Friends/Family of Friends

PLAY

Favorite Social Activities

PLAY

Exercises

PLAY

Vacation/Recreation History

PLAY

People and Places to Avoid

PLAY

Other

WORSHIP

Place of Worship

WORSHIP

Spiritual Leader and Staff

WORSHIP

Desired Religious Education

IMPORTANT DATES TO REMEMBER

PARENT/GUARDIAN INSIGHT

EMERGENCY CONTACTS

GLOSSARY OF TERMS

Accommodations (a.k.a. reasonable accommodations), assistance or changes to a position or workplace that enables an employee to do his or her job despite having a disability. Required under the ADA.

Adaptive technologies (or "assistive" technologies), any "product, device or equipment, whether acquired commercially, modified or customized, that is used to maintain, increase or improve the functional capabilities of an individual's disabilities."

Advocacy, the act of pleading for, supporting, or recommending

Applied behavior analysis, the process of systematically applying interventions based upon the principles of learning theory to improve socially significant behaviors to a meaningful degree, and to demonstrate that the interventions employed are responsible for the improvement in behavior. http://eden2.org/what-is-applied-behavior-analysis/

Asperger Syndrome, a developmental disorder related to autism and characterized by higher than average intellectual ability coupled with impaired social skills and restrictive, repetitive patterns of interest and activities.

Auditory Integration Therapy, an alternative treatment for children who have trouble processing what they hear. https://www.understood.org/en/learning-attention-issues/treatments-approaches/therapies/auditory-training-therapy-what-it-is-and-how-it-works

Autism spectrum, any of a group of developmental disorders marked by impairments in the ability to communicate and interact socially and by the presence of repetitive behaviors or restricted interests (also known as pervasive developmental disorder). https://www.nimh.nih.gov/health/topics/autism-spectrum-disorders-ask/index.shtml

Autism Spectrum Disorder, a condition related to brain development that impacts how a person perceives and socializes with others, causing problems in social interaction and communication, and includes limited and repetitive patterns of behavior.

Echolalia, a psychiatric term used to describe what some people with mental disorders or autism tend to do, automatically repeating what they hear other people say, or a mechanical echoing of sounds.

Floortime, a relationship-based therapy for children with autism in which a parent gets down on the floor with the child to play and interact with the child at their level.

High School Transition Plan, the section of the IEP that outlines transition goals and services for a student, based on a high school student's individual needs, strengths, skills and interests.

I.E.P., Individualized Education Program, https://www.understood.org/en/school-learning/special-services/ieps/understanding-individualized-education-programs

In force Illustration, a picture of your insurance policy as it stands now, which will show the exact results of what has happened from the initial policy inception to today with future projections based on current assumptions.

Intensive listening therapy, activities that focus the student's attention on language form to raise the learners' awareness of how differences in sound, structure, and lexical choice can affect meaning.

Person-first-language, emphasizes the person, not the disability, thereby no longer making the disability the primary consideration, depicting several aspects of the whole person.

Pervasive Development Disorders - a group of disorders characterized by delays in the develoɔment of socialization and communication skills. Symptoms may occur as early as infancy, with the typical age of onset before 3 years of age.

Quantitative Research, a structured way of collecting and analyzing data obtained from different sources, involving the use of computational, statistical and mathematical tools to obtain results.

Qualitative Research, a scientific method of observation to gather non-numerical data.

Relationship Development Intervention (RDI), family-based, behavioral treatment that addresses the core symptoms of autism, focusing on building social and emotional skills. Parents are trained as the primary therapists in most RDI programs. https://www.rdiconnect.com/about-rdi/

Sensory Integration Therapy, a technique used by occupational therapists (OTs) to change how the brain reacts to touch, sound, sight and movement. https://harkla.co/blogs/special-needs/sensory-integration-therapy

Third Party Special Needs Trust, set up by a donor who contributes the funds to the trust typically designed as part of the donor's estate plan to help a member with special needs while the donor is still living, and to manage an inheritance for the person with special needs when the donor dies. www.specialneedsanswers.com

Tomatis Listening Therapy, most comprehensive and effective technology of all existing auditory stimulation programs. https://www.kidslanguagearts.com/tomatis-listening-therapy

RECOMMENDED READINGS

The Child with Special Needs: Encouraging Intellectual and Emotional Growth, (Stanley Greenspan and Serena Weider) (1998)

Don't Sweat the Small Stuff, (Robert Eliot)

All My Life's a Circle, (Marsha Forest, Jack Pearpoint)

Making Self Employment Work for People with Disabilities, Cary Griffin and David Hammis.

Chantal Sicile-Kira is the author of numerous books on autism, including:

Autism Spectrum Disorder: The complete Guide to Understanding Autism

A Full Life with Autism: From Learning to Forming Relationships to Achieving Independence

Autism Life Skills: 10 Essential Abilities Your Child with Autism Needs to Learn

A complete list of her books can be found by Googling "Chantal Sicile-Kira"

RESOURCES

ABLE Act - Achieving a Better Life Experience Act of 2013 (ABLE Act) www.onefpa.org/Journal/Pages

ABLE Accounts - http://www.ablenrc.org/about/what-are-able-accounts

ABLE National Resource Center, www.ABLENRC.org

Academy of Special Needs Planners, a nationwide network of attorneys and financial planners who provide special needs planning services to families and organizations (https.specialneedsanswers.com)

ADVICE is a partnership between NEXT for AUTISM, Autism Speaks, key businesses, community organizations and a team of National Business Disability Consultants. www.Autism-Advice.org

A Guide to Disability Rights Laws (2009), https://www.ada.gov/cguide.htm

Americans with Disabilities Act of 1990 (ADA), a civil rights law prohibiting discrimination against individuals with disabilities in all areas of public life, including jobs, schools, transportation and all public and private places that are open to the general public. https://www.eeoc.gov/eeoc/history/35th/1990s/ada.html

Autism After 16, provides information and analysis of adult autism issues, with the emphasis on analysis (www.autismafter16.com)

Autism CARES Act 2014, the Combating Autism Reauthorization Act of 2014, or Autism Collaboration, Accountability, Research, Education and Support Act of 2014, that amends the public health service act to continue important investments in research, prevalence monitoring and services for both children and adults on the autism spectrum. https://www.congress.gov/bill/113th-congress/senate-bill/2449

Autism Society of America, nation's leading grassroots autism organization, http://www.autism-society.org

Autism Speaks, provides advice on locating providers for assistance with issues of autism. https://www.autismspeaks.org/

Autistic Self Advocacy Network, seeks to advance the principles of the disability rights movement with regard to autism and believes the goal of autism advocacy should be a world in which autistic people enjoy equal access, rights and opportunities. https://autisticadvocacy.org/

Autonomy Works, leverages the talents of people with autism with attention to detail, focus through repetitive tasks, and dedication to quality thereby freeing companies from the burden of repetitive processing work. www.autonomy.works

Bureau of Developmental Disabilities Services (State of Indiana) https://www.in.gov/fssa/ddrs/2639.htm

Center for Autism and Related Disorders (CARD), worldwide organization using Applied Behavioral Analysis (ABA) in the treatment of autism spectrum disorder. https://www.centerforautism.com

Center for Disease Control Autism (CDC), committed to providing essential data on ASD, search for factors that put children at risk for ASD, and possible causes, and to develop resources that help identify children with ASD as early as possible. https://www.cdc.gov/ncbddd/autism/index.html

Consumer Federation of America, non-profit organization founded in 1968 to advance consumer interests through research, education and advocacy. www.consumerfed.org

Family and Social Services Administration (State of Indiana) https://www.in.gov/fssa/

Health Care, site to apply for 2019 plans and services, www.healthcare.gov

Interagency Autism Coordinating Committee, U.S. federal advisory panel with the Department of Health and Human Services (HHS) coordinating efforts within HHS concerning autism spectrum disorder. https://iacc.hhs.gov

Illinois Early Intervention Training Program (EITP), provides training opportunities for early intervention professionals in Illinois, funded by the Illinois Department of Human Services Bureau of Early Intervention to develop a system that is regionalized, responsive and reflective of best practice in the field of early intervention in Illinois. https://eitp.education.illinois.edu

Life Happens, formerly the LIFE Foundation, a nonprofit organization dedicated to helping Americans take personal financial responsibility through the ownership of life insurance and related products, including disability and long-term care insurance. www.lifehappens.org

Mental Health & Autism Insurance Project, a non-profit formed to assist families with children with autism spectrum disorders and/or other mental health conditions to obtain medically necessary treatments through their health plans. Nationwide service. www.mhautism.org

National PLAN Alliance, non-profit organization dedicated solely to meeting the planning needs of families with adult children having lifelong disabilities. www.nationalplanalliance.org

National Conference of State Legislatures, www.ncsl.org

National Disability Institute, an alliance of organizations and individuals dedicated to a common mission for the economic advancement of people with disabilities. https://www.realeconomicimpact.org

PUNS – Prioritization of Urgency of Need for Services, Illinois database to identify and plan for immediate needs, www.dhs.state.il.us

Rehabilitation Act of 1973, prohibits discrimination on the basis of disability in programs conducted by federal agencies, in programs receiving federal financial assistance, in federal employment and in the employment practices of federal contractors. https://www.ada.gov/cguide.htm

Special Needs Trust Administration, organization assisting in establishing trusts by the beneficiary or someone acting on their behalf with the beneficiary's funds for the purpose of retaining or obtaining eligibility for public benefits. https://www.specialneedsalliance.org/wp-content/uploads/2016/04/2016-Handbook-for-Trustees.pdf

Special Needs Alliance, national organization comprised of attorneys committed to helping individuals with disabilities, their families and the professionals who serve them. www.specialneedsalliance.org

SSI – Supplemental Security Income, www.ssa.gov.

Title XVI SSI for the Aged, Blind, and Disabled of the Social Security Act, disability benefits administered by the Social Security Administration, https://www.disabilitybenefitscenter.org/glossary/title-xvi-benefits

Waisman Center, University of Wisconsin—Madison, program entitled University Center for Excellence in Developmental Disabilities www.waismanucedd.wiscweb.wisc.edu

ABOUT THE AUTHORS

Gregory M. Zibricky, CFP®, ChFC, CLU, CASL

Greg is recognized and regarded for his expertise in the fields of Financial and Special Needs Planning. He has over 33 years of experience helping clients identify the financial strategies that will work best for them. As a parent of a child with Autism, he brings exceptional awareness and a unique perspective to his work.

Featured in *Financial Advisor Magazine*, the article "A Special Dedication" focused on Greg's commitment to the families of special needs children. Greg has also been quoted in the *Chicago Tribune, Chicago Sun Times, Chicago Magazine, Investment News,* and *Exceptional Parent.*

Greg has spoken at many national and regional conferences including the Autism Society of America, Capital Trust Symposium, and at the Cambridge Investment Research National Conference.

Greg graduated with a degree in Business Administration with distinction from Lewis University. He has earned the professional designations of Certified Financial Planner (CFP®), Chartered Financial Consultant (ChFC), Chartered Life Underwriter (CLU) and Chartered Advisor for Senior Living (CASL).

C. Dawn Zibricky, Ed.D., RN, PEL-CSN

Dawn Zibricky received both baccalaureate and master's degrees from Saint Xavier University in Chicago and a doctoral degree in Educational Leadership for Teaching and Learning from Lewis University in Romeoville, Illinois. Her extensive nursing career includes working with individuals in rehabilitation for traumatic injuries, people with disabilities, and individuals and families living in rural, urban and suburban poverty both in the US and globally. As a nurse educator, Dawn is dedicated to guiding students in developing awareness about health and health care disparities and promoting social justice.

Dawn's research interests include disability studies framed in critical theories and teaching ethics in nursing education. She has presented both nationally and internationally on the oppression and marginalization of the disabled, poverty, and health care disparities.

Prior to obtaining her doctorate degree, Dawn specialized in the care of persons with traumatic brain injuries and spinal cord injuries. She served as nurse consultant for Lincoln-Way Area Special Education Cooperative integrating children with various disabilities into the school setting. Inspired by her oldest son Aaron, who has autism, Dawn has worked as a regional trainer of autism through the Illinois Autism/PDD Training and Technical Assistance program since 1977. She is a nationally respected speaker on many topics including the autism spectrum, parenting, and children with disabilities in the school setting and person-centered planning.

Dawn is a member of numerous professional memberships including Sigma Theta Tau International Honor Society of Nursing, Delta Kappa Gamma Society International of Women Educators, Phi Delta Kappa International Honor Society for Educators and Kappa Delta Pi International Honor Society in Education.

CONTACT INFORMATION

Greg Zibricky
Provider Group Wealth Advisors
Phone: 630-789-6313
E-Mail: greg@providergroup.com
Web: www.providergroup.com

Securities offered through Cambridge Investment Research, Inc. a Broker/Dealer, Member FINRA/SIPC, Investment Advisor Representative, Cambridge Investment Research Advisors, Inc., a Registered Investment Advisor. Cambridge and Provider Group, Ltd. are not affiliated.

35494220R00070

Made in the USA
Lexington, KY
04 April 2019